Contents

About the authors

Mathew Brown is an experienced teacher and currently a Director of ICT and E-Learning. He is passionate about graphics and design.

Kenny Sharpe is a Curriculum Leader at Sussex Coast College with several years experience of teaching BTEC Information Technology across all levels of the academic structure.

Credits

The publisher would like to thank the following for their kind permission to reproduce their photographs:

(Key: b-bottom; c-centre; l-left; r-right; t-top)

Alamy Images: Alex Segre 1, Blend Images 113, Blue Jean Images 22, Buddy Mays 16, Christy Varonfakis Johnson 79, Format1 83, ICP-UK 124, Image Source 82, Jeff Morgan 06 123, Kevin Britland 106, mcx images 139, Melissa Ferrari 62, NetPics 52, ONOKY – Photononstop 191, Pablo Paul 74, Patrick La Roque 89, Per Karlsson-BKWine.com 104, Raine Varu 48, Stocksearch 27, Westend61 GmbH 198; **Corbis:** Rick Gomez 186; **Getty Images:** AFP / Jonathan UTZ 102, Imagebank 196; **iStockphoto:** Mike Manzana 65; **Masterfile UK Ltd:** Straus / Curtis 177; **Pearson Education Ltd:** Jules Selmes 192; **Photoshot Holdings Limited:** YM YIK 55; **Shutterstock.com:** 300dpi 3, Alessandro Zocc 60, alphaspirit 181, AVAVA 68, Christina Richards 4, dani3315 59, diagon 56b, Dmitry Rukhlenko 10, Fenton 8, greenland 194, Ilja Masik 167, Inga Nielsen 21, iodrakon 81, Kilson 45, Kwest 95t, 95b, LeNi 179, Masalski Maksim 92tl, michahoerichs 91, Monkey Business Images 189, Nikolay Khoroshkov 101, Penham James Mitchinson 108, Rob Marmion 13, Ronen 42, RT Images 15, Rudyanto Wijaya 168, stoyanh 56c, Supri Suharjoto 118, Svemir 19, Tatiana Popova 56t, 58, Tyler Olsen 76, Yuri Arcurs 7, ZTS 24, 92tr, zurijeta 98

Cover images: *Front:* **SuperStock:** Glow Images; *Back:* **Shutterstock.com:** Monkey Business Images tl, Svemir tr

All other images © Pearson Education

Picture Research by: Chrissie Martin

We are grateful to the following for permission to reproduce copyright material:

p.153 Twitter screenshot reprinted with permission from Twitter.
Unit E20, Serif PhotoPlus screenshots reprinted with permission from Serif.
p.161 Apple iTunes screenshot reprinted with permission from Apple.

Microsoft product screenshots reprinted with permission from Microsoft Corporation.

Every effort has been made to trace the copyright holders and we apologise in advance for any unintentional omissions. We would be pleased to insert the appropriate acknowledgement in any subsequent edition of this publication.

About your BTEC Entry 3/Level 1 IT Users

Choosing to study for a BTEC Entry 3 or Level 1 IT Users qualification is a great decision to make for lots of reasons. Information Technology (IT) is an exciting area. It is constantly expanding into areas of our everyday life. It is hard to imagine our lives without IT.

IT is never far from the news. Perhaps it is a launch of a new product like the iPad, or perhaps a new development in social networking. IT is always changing, and plays an important role in our everyday lives.

As IT grows, with it comes great opportunities to learn and develop. Jobs are created in these new and exciting areas, and people are needed who have the necessary qualifications and experiences. IT is a rewarding sector to work in, and can be a fulfilling and enjoyable career choice.

Your BTEC Entry 3/Level 1 IT Users is a **vocational** or **work-related** qualification. It will give you the chance to gain knowledge, understanding and skills that are important in the subject or area of work you have chosen.

What will you be doing?

This book covers enough units for you to gain any of the following qualifications:

- BTEC Entry 3 **Award** for IT Users

- BTEC Level 1 **Award** for IT Users

- BTEC Level 1 **Certificate** for IT Users

- BTEC Level 1 **Diploma** for IT Users.

If you are unsure your tutor will let you know what level of qualification you are aiming for.

How to use this book

This book is designed to help you through your BTEC Entry 3/Level 1 IT Users course. It is divided into 16 units to match the units in the specification. Each unit is broken down into smaller topics.

This book contains many features that will help you get the most from your course.

Introduction

Each unit starts with a page that gives you a snapshot of what you will be learning from that unit.

USING MOBILE IT DEVICES | UNIT 108

It is likely that you already own and use a mobile phone for texting, making telephone calls and taking photos. However, many mobile devices available today are capable of doing much more.

Mobile devices are taking an increasingly large role in day-to-day business. This unit will provide you with an insight into the professional capabilities of mobile devices.

Mobile devices are not only phones – they can be personal digital assistants (PDAs), portable media players and electronic organisers.

In this unit you will learn to:

- Set up a mobile device
- Use applications and files
- Transfer data
- Keep the device working well

Is this more than just a mobile phone?

Activities

You will find activities throughout the book. These will help you understand the information in the unit and give you a chance to try things for yourself.

Activity: Effects

Investigate what 'effects' you can use within the software. Try and make the head's skin colour as close to the body's skin colour as you can. It will take some time to experiment with all the different options. (HINT: Look into the Effects options > Image Adjustments.)

Case studies

Case studies show you how what you are learning will help you in the real world of work.

Case study:
Parveen's spam problem

Parveen has an email account. He uses it about once a week to read emails from friends. Recently he has found that every time he opens the account there are loads of emails from strange email addresses, including ones that seem to come from his own email account!

Parveen is really suspicious and deletes all the messages straightaway. He has heard about how you can get viruses by opening emails like this. But the emails keep coming and eventually Parveen stops using the account.

Functional skills

Useful pointers showing you where you can improve your skills in English, Mathematics and ICT.

Functional skills

Learning to use appropriate 'netiquette' when creating formal emails will help develop your skills in **English**.

Key terms

The words you need to understand are easy to spot, and their meanings are clearly explained.

> **✳ Key term**
>
> **Shapes**
> Simple shapes that are used to help improve images, such as magazine covers.

Remember!

Look out for these boxes. They point out really important information.

> **❗ Remember**
>
> Use your address book as much as you can.

Check

You'll find a reminder of key information at the end of each topic.

> **✓ Check**
> - Adding basic shapes can enhance a magazine cover.
> - Text can help the image stand out, and help catch your audience's attention.

Assessment page

This page will help you check what you have done so far and give you tips for getting the best mark you can for each task.

Assessment overview

This table shows you what assessment criteria you need to meet to pass the unit and on which pages you will find activities and information to help you prepare for your assignments.

Edexcel's assignment tips

At the end of each unit, you'll find hints and tips that will help you get the best mark you can.

Your book is just part of the exciting resources from Edexcel to help you succeed in your BTEC course. Visit www.edexcel.com/BTEC or www.pearsonfe.co.uk/BTEC2010 for more details.

BTEC BTEC's own resources

ASSESSMENT OVERVIEW

While working through this unit, you will have prepared for completing the following tasks:

○	1.1	Identify the purpose for using IT	Pages 2–3
○	1.2	Identify the methods, skills and resources required to complete the task successfully	Pages 4–5
○	1.3	Plan how to carry out the task using IT to achieve the required purpose and outcome	Pages 6–7
○	1.4	Identify reasons for choosing particular IT systems and software applications for the task	Pages 6–7
○	1.5	Identify any legal or local guidelines or constraints that may affect the task or activity	Pages 8–9
○	1.6	Select IT systems and software applications as appropriate for the purpose	Pages 10–11
○	2.1	Identify automated routines to improve productivity	Pages 10–11
○	2.2	Use automated routines to aid efficient processing or presentation	Pages 10–11
○	2.3	Complete planned tasks using IT	Pages 10–11
○	3.1	Review outcomes to make sure they meet the requirements of the task and are fit for purpose	Pages 12–13
○	3.2	Decide whether the IT tools selected were appropriate for the task and purpose	Pages 12–13
○	3.3	Identify the strengths and weaknesses of the completed task	Pages 12–13
○	3.4	Identify ways to make further improvements to work	Pages 12–13

edexcel :::

Assignment tips

- Practise writing down the requirements of any task your teacher sets. This will help you plan and organise your work.
- Research different guidelines surrounding the IT sector. You could research the Data Protection Act or the Copyright Act.
- Practice using shortcut keys to speed up your work.
- Find out the strengths and weaknesses of different applications you use every day.

IMPROVING PRODUCTIVITY USING IT

This unit explores how you can improve productivity using computing and IT.

You can use computers to make your life easier. They can allow you to do a lot more in the same space of time. This is known as improving productivity. Information Technology (IT) can be used in many different ways to help a computer user.

IT systems can be expensive and take time to produce, so it is very important to get the most out of any system.

In this unit you will:

- Plan what IT systems and software to use

- Use IT effectively to complete tasks

- Learn to look back over your choices to make sure they were successful

Do you think IT can improve the productivity of a business?

What IT should you use?

IT has a broad range of uses. When deciding which IT system to use, it is very important to carefully think through every stage before the project is started. It is necessary to fully understand what is required from the system. This is its purpose.

Key terms

IT system
A process that is run and operated by a computer.

Purpose
The reason behind doing something (for example, an IT system).

What do you need to think about?	Why?	An example...
Who and what the information is for.	This lets you do things at the right level.	A financial system needs to be very professional, but a calculator for young children needs to be exciting and interactive.
When it must be finished.	So the job gets done on time.	If a business wants to get an IT system up and running on a certain day they will rely on the job being finished.
What information needs to be included.	This shows how the system should be designed.	Simple data like a list of addresses needs a simple system. More complex data needs a more complicated system.
Where it will be used.	Being aware of this will help to plan the system better.	The IT needs of an office will be different to the IT needs of a home.

Once you understand the above questions you can start to plan the system. Planning is very important and will give us a step-by-step approach on how to develop the new system in the most effective manner. You will explore planning in the next topic.

A simple computer system

Activity: Think

What are the main things you need to think about before you start planning which IT system to use?

Check

- You can use IT for a number of reasons.

- It is important to be clear about the reasons for using an IT system before starting a project.

Planning an IT system

It is very important to **plan**. A plan sets a path for people to follow when they are carrying out a project. Planning the project involves breaking down the overall large task into several smaller tasks.

Each step of the plan should be put into a suitable order. You should also think about how long each step will take. You need to think about the following questions:

1. What information sources are needed?

You need to know where you are getting the information from.

2. What application software will be used?

It will save time if you know which software applications you are going to use. Further tips about this can be found in Unit 112.

3. What skills and resources are needed to complete the task successfully?

In larger projects you may need special equipment and/or people with more advanced skills to help.

Key term

Plan
To work out what you need to do before you do it.

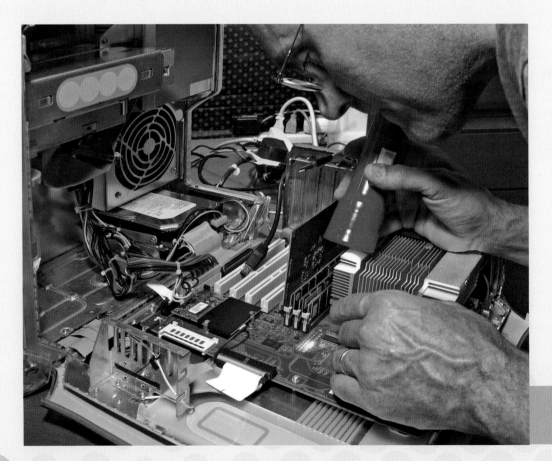

When might you need to contact an IT engineer?

4. Content

You will need to be clear about where and how you are going to use the information you find.

5. Structure and layout

You can plan what something is going to look like and how it will fit together.

6. Timelines

You need to understand what tasks need to be completed and by when. You also need to think about the order you are going to do them in. Some tasks need doing quicker than others.

The above outlines what, where, when and how you are going to achieve the completion of the project. It is also important to understand why decisions are made – you need to be very clear about the reasons why you should use a particular IT system for your project. We will explore this in the next topic.

Activity: Produce a plan

Produce a plan (a list is fine) for a trip to the local cinema. Break it down into as many smaller steps as you can.

Check

- Planning is a breakdown of one big task into several smaller ones.

- Planning is an essential stage of any system development.

Deciding on using an IT system

Anyone who plans to build an IT system needs to be very clear about the reasons for producing the system before they start. This is very important because building an IT system could work out to be very expensive. Below are some considerations to take into account:

- Time: an IT system should save time. This will increase productivity of the work force.

- Convenience: will the system be helpful? Does the new system make things easier for the person who is going to use it?

- Cost: how much will the system cost? Taking the cost into account, will the system save the company money in the long run?

- Benefits of IT in comparison to manual methods: both manual and IT methods have advantages and disadvantages. It is important to understand and compare all of these before making a choice about whether to use an IT system.

- Quality: will the system add value to the company or organisation? Will an IT system improve the situation?

- Accuracy: the system needs to be 100% accurate. Computer systems will produce very few mistakes if they are set up correctly in the beginning. Humans, on the other hand, will always make mistakes.

Streamlining business processes

As well as all the considerations above, setting up IT systems can help businesses to run more smoothly and efficiently (to streamline). A computing system could replace a manual task with the click of a button. This will save a lot of time and money in the long term.

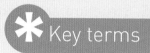

Key terms

Accuracy
The level of how closely something matches its required state.

Streamline
To ensure that different elements of a business work together in a smoother and more efficient manner

Case study:
IT solutions

Charlie is an IT development manager and works for a clothing retailer. The company want to improve their ordering system because they are taking more and more orders. This is putting a lot of strain on the staff as many of the orders are being processed manually. Also, members of staff sometimes make mistakes when they are writing down orders, meaning that orders can go missing.

The director of the company asks Charlie to come up with a solution to this problem using IT. Charlie begins looking into the matter to see if IT will help. He decides to use a spreadsheet created using Microsoft Excel® to log orders. This will save time and stop customers' orders going missing. It will also mean there is a record of all the orders.

Activity: Think

What else do you think an IT system would help with in this situation?

Check

- It is very important to decide on the benefits of using an IT system before building one.

- An IT system can save a lot of time but may cost a lot of money to set up.

Guidelines and constraints

Anyone developing an IT system needs to stick within the **constraints** and **guidelines** set out by the law and the company they are working for. Otherwise it could cost a lot of time and money to put right.

Data protection

The Data Protection Act (1998) protects you and I from other people using our data inappropriately. System designers must ensure that they follow the Act when using other people's data.

Activity: Researching

Search for 'Data Protection Act 1998' in a search engine of your choice. See what you can find out about it.

Copyright

The Copyright Act means that people can't use other people's work without their permission. It is important that you seek permission from the original owner before using their work.

Software licensing

Each piece of software that you use on your computer must have a licence. The company that built and owns the software will want users to sign a licence agreement before using it.

Security

When using sensitive data (such as financial details) it is important that only the intended audience can view the information. One method of making a system more secure is to add a password.

✱ Key terms

Constraints
Rules that we are not allowed to break.

Guidelines
Suggestions about how to do things.

Functional skills

Searching for information to read on the Internet will improve your skills in **ICT** and **English**.

House style

Most companies will have their own logo and normally use the same house style on all of their products. This includes using a certain font at a particular size. House style will also usually consist of particular colours. The computer system is likely to use the same style. When working for a particular company, you must ensure that you stick to their house style.

* Key term

House style
Set colours, logos and fonts used by an organisation.

Activity: Group discussion

Make a list of the guidelines and constraints that you would need to think about if you were designing a company website.

Check

- It is a legal requirement to abide by the Data Protection Act.

- Each company will have its own guidelines and styles.

Automated routines

Today, technology is becoming more and more advanced. Advances in technology mean that using a computer or IT system has become easier.

Complex tasks are carried out by computers at the click of a button. These complex tasks have been created by programmers and stored on the computer. The task will only be carried out if and when the button is clicked. This is known as an automated routine.

Shortcut menus

Shortcut menus can save you a lot of time. Shortcuts mean that an event that would take several seconds to perform can be carried out at the press of two buttons. Normally (but not always) you will have to press and hold the control key and then another to trigger one of these shortcuts.

✱ Key terms

Automated routine
A pre-recorded event that will occur when a certain action is performed (for example, a press of a button).

Icon
A simple picture that indicates a program or a command.

Activity: Using shortcut keys

Try the following shortcut keys and make note of what they do in Microsoft Word®:

- Ctrl + a
- Ctrl + c
- Ctrl + f
- Ctrl + p
- Ctrl + s.

Customised menus and toolbars

The toolbar can be found in most office-based applications.

Icons (small pictures) on the toolbar are used as shortcuts to different options available within the software. You can change which icons are available on the toolbar. This allows you to choose the icons that are the most useful for your needs.

You can change which icons are available on the toolbar. For example, in Microsoft Word® you can click 'Tools' then 'Customize' and choose the icons you want.

Macros

Macros are a pre-recorded set of events that run when a certain event takes place. For example, a macro could be created to open a specific file.

Templates

Templates take different forms. Examples include pre-created software that has been created by another person for us to use, or the outline of a new document.

Activity: Think

Think of a few automated routines that you use all the time on a computer. Are there any others you could practise using?

Check

- Automated routines can save the user a lot of valuable time.
- Templates can be used more than once.

Reviewing an IT system

Once an IT system has been created, it should be checked to make sure that it is ready for the end user. This means checking that it will carry out the tasks it is expected to do. The system must be **tested** and **reviewed** before the end user uses it.

Reviewing requirements

Anyone building a new system needs to be clear about its requirements from the start. It is very important to keep thinking about these requirements as the system progresses and also to check when the system is finished that the requirements have been met.

IT tools selection

When an IT system is complete, it can be very helpful to review the tools used. This way, valuable knowledge can be gained about which tools are best for which tasks. Tools can be reviewed by thinking about the following points:

- Time taken
- Convenience
- Cost
- Quality
- Accuracy.

Strengths and weaknesses of an IT system

In order to identify the strengths and weaknesses of an IT system, you can look at how well the following things worked:

- Format: the structure of a system. How things link together and work together.
- Layout: how something looks. Think about colour and where things are positioned within the system.
- Accuracy: does the system work correctly? It is important that an IT system does what it sets out to do.
- Clarity for audience: is the system clear and easy for the user to use? If the system is very complex to use it may not be used as much as expected.

Improvements

A system may be up and in place and it may do the job that meets the requirements stated at the beginning of the project. Nevertheless, there are always likely to be improvements in any piece of software or application. It is possible to:

- correct mistakes

- think of better ways of doing things

- learn new techniques.

What may be obvious to one person may confuse another.

Activity: Review an IT system

Think of a few automated routines that you use all the time on a computer. Are there any others you could practise using?

Check

- IT systems can be improved by carrying out a review.

- The strengths and weaknesses of an IT system can be highlighted as part of the review process.

ASSESSMENT OVERVIEW

While working through this unit, you will have prepared for completing the following tasks:

○	1.1	Identify the purpose for using IT	Pages 2–3
○	1.2	Identify the methods, skills and resources required to complete the task successfully	Pages 4–5
○	1.3	Plan how to carry out the task using IT to achieve the required purpose and outcome	Pages 6–7
○	1.4	Identify reasons for choosing particular IT systems and software applications for the task	Pages 6–7
○	1.5	Identify any legal or local guidelines or constraints that may affect the task or activity	Pages 8–9
○	1.6	Select IT systems and software applications as appropriate for the purpose	Pages 10–11
○	2.1	Identify automated routines to improve productivity	Pages 10–11
○	2.2	Use automated routines that aid efficient processing or presentation	Pages 10–11
○	2.3	Complete planned tasks using IT	Pages 10–11
○	3.1	Review outcomes to make sure they meet the requirements of the task and are fit for purpose	Pages 12–13
○	3.2	Decide whether the IT tools selected were appropriate for the task and purpose	Pages 12–13
○	3.3	Identify the strengths and weaknesses of the completed task	Pages 12–13
○	3.4	Identify ways to make further improvements to work	Pages 12–13

edexcel

Assignment tips

- Practise writing down the requirements of any task your tutor sets. This will help you plan and organise your work.

- Research different guidelines surrounding the IT sector. You could research the Data Protection Act or the Copyright Act.

- Practise using shortcut keys to speed up your work.

- Find out the strengths and weaknesses of different applications you use every day.

There are many different aspects to IT.

Understanding how a computer works is very important to a career in IT. However, understanding that different people have different levels of ability is also very important.

In your IT career, you may be asked to set up an IT system where you need to take the users' needs into account.

In this unit, you will:

- Learn how an IT system meets its users' needs

- Learn how to organise, store and find information

- Learn about safety and security when using IT

- Learn how to deal with IT system problems and maintain IT systems

Are you able to identify problems with computers and user needs?

IT systems to meet needs

IT systems

Most IT systems need users to **log in** to be able to access and use the system.

Users will need to 'log in' with their user name and password. This allows the system to restrict who is allowed to use the system. You can also lock a computer, so no one else can use it while you are logged in. This is handy if you need to leave your computer but don't want to log out.

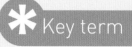

Key term

Log in
Logging into a computer or system with an individual user name and password.

◎ Activity: Group discussion

Why might you want to control who can log into your system?

Interface features

User interface refers to the software that you ('the user') use when you use a computer system. The interface allows users to work with the computer. Examples of user interfaces include the following:

- Scrollbars

- Toolbars

- Icons

- Buttons

- Zoom

- Minimise/maximise.

Once a user is familiar with these features, they can use the system effectively.

Key term

User interface
Software to enable/help users to work with a computer.

Have you tried changing your desktop wallpaper?

Customising user interfaces

When you use your computer at home, you may want to start customising it. This means changing the settings to the way you want them. You could change the desktop wallpaper, the size and colour of icons, or even the size of the screen (**screen resolution**).

Key term

Screen resolution
How much detail is displayed on a computer monitor.

By changing some of these things, you are actually customising the user interface.

Some users may have very different needs than you, and may require a level of customisation that perhaps you wouldn't find so useful.

Activity: Group discussion

What kind of customisation would you use for a user who is visually impaired (i.e. has trouble with seeing)?

Communication services

Communication services meet another user need by allowing users to connect to the Internet.

This can be through various connection methods:

- Broadband (DSL)

- Dial up (56K modem)

- Wireless (wi-fi)

- Mobile networks (mobile phones/dongles).

Activity: Scenario

Imagine you work in an office and need to go out for the day, but still need to have access to the Internet. Out of the methods listed above, which one(s) could you use?

Check

- IT systems have several features to make them easier to use.

- You can change the settings of the system to suit the user.

Key terms

DSL
A telephone line that has special equipment which allows it to receive information from the Internet, or send information at very high speeds.

Modem
A piece of electronic equipment that allows information from one computer to be sent along telephone wires to another computer.

Wi-fi
A way of connecting computers or other electronic machines to a network by using radio signals rather than wires.

Dongle
An electronic device that is plugged into the computer to allow a copy-protected program to run.

Describing IT systems

IT systems vary in their set-up. Here are some examples of different IT systems:

- Personal computer (PC/Mac)
- Laptop (PC/Mac)
- Tablet (iPad/Dell)
- Mobile devices (Android/Apple/Windows).

Using the right term

IT systems have common terms to describe their parts. 'Input' covers ways of putting information into the system. 'Output' covers the ways that information comes out.

Input	Output
Keyboard	Printer
Mouse	Speakers
CD/DVD	Screen
Scanner	

Key terms

Input
How information is put into a computer.

Output
How a computer gives out information.

Central Processing Unit (CPU)
The CPU is the 'brain' of the IT system. It is the central processing point for all information and activity in the system.

Functional skills

Understanding the correct terms for IT systems will help you improve your skills in English.

Case study:
Technical terms

Skye works in the IT department of a large design agency in London. He helps members of staff outside the IT department who are having problems with their computer systems.

Sometimes Skye finds that the people that call him with problems don't understand him when he uses technical terms like 'input device'. This makes it hard for him to work out the problem they are having. There is a communication problem.

He tries to think of ways around this. In the end he makes a table with the main technical terms he uses and then puts a simple word or phrase next to them that he knows his colleagues will understand.

Activity: Simplifying

Create a table and in the first column put a list of the main technical terms you have learned so far. Try and think of a simple way of saying each term and put this in the next column. Try them out on your friends or relatives to see if they make sense.

Check

- There are many different IT system set-ups.

- There are special words you need to learn to describe the parts of IT systems.

Organise, store and retrieve information

File and folder handling

Organising your **digital files** will help when you are trying to find something on your computer later.

Think of a computer as a massive filing cabinet. Within that filing cabinet, you have folders. Creating digital **folders** makes finding things much easier, and quicker. Just like a filing cabinet sorted alphabetically (A to Z).

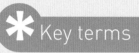

Key terms

Digital file
A file that is created when you create and save work on a computer.

Folder
A digital folder that helps you to organise digital files on a computer.

Activity: Think

How do you think a hotel would organise their filing cabinet of customers' details?

- By last name
- By first name
- By telephone number.

Moving files

Moving files is quite a simple task. You can simply 'drag and drop' a file by clicking on the file icon, holding the mouse button down, and dragging the file to where you want it.

Deleting files

Deleting files is even easier. Simply click once on a file icon and hit the delete key. (You can also right click, and choose the 'Delete' option.)

When you delete a file, it goes into a 'Trash' or 'Recycle' bin. You can restore deleted files from this bin. (A bit like an 'Undo' option.)

Activity: Deleting and restoring

Delete a file, then visit your 'Trash' or 'Recycle' bin – see if you can 'restore' the file.

Storage media

You can 'back up' your files by copying them onto storage media. Types of storage media include:

- USB pen drive

- CD/DVD

- External hard drive.

These are known as 'portable' storage media, meaning you can easily move and carry your files with you.

Storage space is measured in MegaBytes (MB) and GigaBytes (GB).

An external hard drive

Activity: Choosing storage media

Which of the storage media above would you use to store a large file like a film?

✓ Check

- Files and folders help you to organise information on your computer.

- You can store material outside your computer with a storage media device.

Safety and security

Work safety

If you work at a computer for a long period of time, you could **risk** putting your body under **physical stress** by repeating certain actions.

When working at a computer, you need to make sure that you are sitting comfortably and, more importantly, sitting up straight and not slouching or bent over. The monitor should be at eye level, and a safe distance. This should help reduce stress and strain on your eyes.

Activity: Think

Can you think of any other **health and safety** tips to bear in mind when working on computers?

Viruses

Viruses can cause all sorts of problems for computers. There are many different types of virus.

Prevention is better than cure and, rather than trying to fix a computer infected with a virus, preventing the virus in the first place makes much more sense. Examples of software that prevent infection include:

- Anti-virus software (these help prevent your computer getting infected by a virus).
- Firewalls (these help prevent any unauthorised intrusion into your computer from the Internet).

Viruses are usually transferred from infected files, such as email attachments, or from files that have been downloaded from unknown sources on the Internet.

Activity: Research

Try to find out exactly how many computer viruses there are in 2010/2011. (HINT: Use a search engine.)

Sitting correctly at a computer

! Remember

Be sure to scan any unknown files with anti-virus software first!

* Key terms

Risk
Potential threats to people's safety.

Physical stress
When the body is under constant use, which could cause harm or injury.

Health and safety
Making sure that people are safe when using a computer.

Information security

Staying safe online involves much more than being aware of your personal safety. You need to think who might see or use your personal information:

- Is your password easy to guess?

- Do you use your real name when online?

- Do you allow everyone to see your Facebook/Bebo/MySpace profile?

- Do you include all of your personal information on your social networking pages?

Guidelines

Guidelines are designed to protect you online, and to protect the organisation where you are using IT equipment. For example, most schools and colleges block access to certain chatrooms. This isn't to stop your fun, but to avoid exposing young adults to potentially dangerous criminals.

Do you know exactly with whom you are chatting to online?

Activity: Think

What do you think criminals could do with your personal information?

Check

- The way that you sit at your computer can affect your physical well-being.

- The Internet can be dangerous – you need to be very careful with your personal details and who you interact with online.

Routine maintenance

Routines

Maintenance of any mechanical components is key to ensuring a long life for the equipment. Completing maintenance regularly (routinely), helps to achieve this. This can done by doing simple things such as:

- Removing dust
- Cleaning parts
- Deleting unwanted files
- Replacing parts
- Running maintenance software.

Printers in particular are often neglected. They need to be regularly cleaned and ink cartridges changed. By doing such basic things, the life of a printer can be extended.

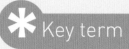
Key term

Maintenance
Cleaning, checking, improving, modifying to ensure something continues to work properly.

Why may it be better to keep a printer on a desk rather than the floor?

Activity: Research

Read a manual of a printer, and check its maintenance guide on how to extend its life. Are there any key features that the manufacturer recommends? (For example, using their own branded inks.)

Advice

Advice is often given freely by many people. You need to be able to identify what advice is valid, and what advice to ignore. The wrong type of advice could be disastrous and cause faults with your hardware.

Experts are usually people with experience or qualifications, and should know what they are talking about.

You could try asking an IT systems support technician. Online IT support message boards can also provide useful advice.

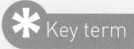
Key term

Advice
Information from someone who has greater knowledge about something.

Guidelines

Manufacturers of hardware will provide guidelines to help keep their hardware in excellent working order. You may need to seek expert advice or read the manufacturers' guidelines, when you reach the limit of your own understanding.

IT problems

The following table outlines some typical IT problems and what you can do about them:

The problem	The cause	How you can fix it
Computer 'freezes', i.e. it locks or does nothing.	Several possible causes.	Hold down the power button for 5–10 seconds until the computer restarts. If the problem continues, seek expert advice.
Mouse or keyboard does not work.	Cable between mouse/ keyboard and computer could be damaged or not plugged in.	Check the cable for each device is properly plugged into the computer.
Your files do not print.	Printer is jammed or out of ink.	Check for paper jams and levels of ink.
You can't log in.	User name and password do not work.	Check you have spelt both correctly. Check the 'Caps Lock' key is not on.
You cannot find your work, or it has been deleted.	Your work hasn't been saved, or has got lost.	Make sure you have checked all locations on the computer, or use the computer's 'search' function. If you still can't find it, seek expert advice.

Activity: Think

What could you do if you lost an important piece of work on your computer?

✓ Check

- Maintenance is vital in order to keep equipment working properly.

- Expert advice and manufacturers' guidelines can help when you have problems.

ASSESSMENT OVERVIEW

While working through this unit, you will have prepared for completing the following tasks:

○ 1.1	Use correct procedures to start and shut down an IT system	Pages 16–17
○ 1.2	Use interface features effectively to interact with IT systems	Pages 16–17
○ 1.3	Adjust system settings to meet individual needs	Pages 16–17
○ 1.4	Use a communication service to access the Internet	Pages 16–17
○ 1.5	Use appropriate terminology when describing IT systems	Pages 18–19
○ 2.1	Work with files and folders so that it is easy to find and retrieve information	Pages 20–21
○ 2.2	Organise and store information, using general and local conventions where appropriate	Pages 20–21
○ 2.3	Identify what storage media to use	Pages 20–21
○ 3.1	Work safely and take steps to minimise physical stress	Pages 22–23
○ 3.2	Recognise the danger of computer viruses and identify ways to minimise risk	Pages 22–23
○ 3.3	Keep information secure	Pages 22–23
○ 3.4	Recognise why it is important to stay safe and to respect others when using IT-based communication	Pages 22–23
○ 3.5	Follow relevant guidelines and procedures for the safe and secure use of IT	Pages 22–23
○ 4.1	Recognise why routine maintenance of hardware is important and when to carry it out	Pages 24–25
○ 4.2	Be aware of where to get expert advice	Pages 24–25
○ 4.3	Carry out regular routine maintenance of hardware and software safely	Pages 24–25
○ 4.4	Take appropriate action to handle routine IT problems	Pages 24–25

edexcel :::

Assignment tips

- Always log off or shut down your computer properly after use.
- Keep your files organised using folders. It makes it easier to find them later.
- Always treat attachments in emails with caution. Scan them with anti-virus software wherever possible.
- Check your hardware components, and routinely do simple things like clean moving parts. (Read the manufacturers' guidelines for expert maintenance advice.)

IT COMMUNICATION FUNDAMENTALS

The Internet provides lots of information for research. However, it is important to be able to tell the difference between the useful and non-useful or inaccurate information when you are faced with pages and pages of potential sources of information.

This unit will develop your ability to find relevant information from the Internet using a search browser, such as Google, Yahoo! and Bing, and exchanging information using email or IT-based communication.

In this unit, you will learn to:

- Identify different sources of information available to you

- Pick out relevant information

- Exchange information using IT

Do you recognise this famous website?

Sources of information

Everywhere you look there are different sources of **information**.

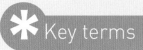

Key terms

Information
Knowledge gained through study, experience or instruction.

Search engine
A program that searches documents for keywords and returns a list of the documents where the keywords were found.

Activity: Different sources of information

How many different sources of information can you think of?

- Newspapers
- Books
- Images
- Maps
- Conversations
- CDs

- DVDs
- Text messages
- Internet
- Podcasts
- Web logs
- **Search engines**.

Did you come up with all of these sources of information?

The source of information you use will depend on the type of information you need to find out about. For example, you wouldn't use a newspaper to find out where in the world a country is, you would use a map instead.

Features of information

You should always think about the features of the information you are using. Is it:

- factual
- creative
- opinion
- continually updated or live
- interactive?

Copyright

When researching information you must consider the appropriate copyright laws. It is important not to copy and present material as if it was your own work. This is known as plagiarism.

You often need to pay for music to download it legally

If you want to download music you should ensure that it is done legally. Downloading music illegally has a negative impact on the company that made the music. Illegal music downloading could mean hefty fines or even being sent to prison.

Activity: Factual information sources

Name a source of information that is likely to provide factual information.

Check

- The sources of information you choose should be based on the type of information you need to find out about.

- Copyright law means you can't copy someone else's work and present it as your own.

Using a search engine

Using search engines

There are a number of search engines available to use on the Internet today. To access a search engine you will need to enter the web address for that particular search engine into the address bar of an Internet browser, such as Internet Explorer, as shown below.

Once you have entered the web address for the search engine's website, the home page for the search engine will appear on screen. All search engines look relatively similar. They all include a big box for you to type in what you are trying to search.

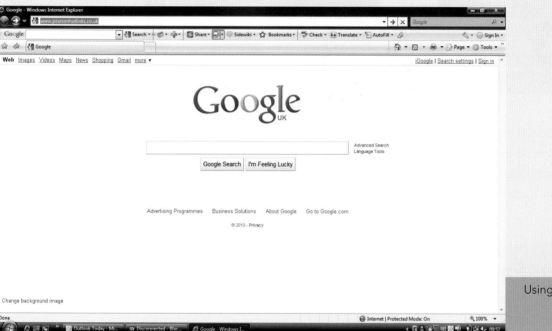

Using a search engine

Once you have entered some **key words** into the search box and pressed 'enter', you will be shown pages containing links to different sources of information. The search engine usually sorts the links according to which it considers to be most **relevant** to your search, and it will display these at the top of the page.

A search engine results page looks like this:

As you can see from the screenshot above, a simple search can provide you with a number of links. Each represents a different source of information available on the Internet.

To view a link from the results page, simply click on the title. As you can see from the screenshot above, this is usually underlined. This will then take you to the website.

Activity: Using search engines

Try using a search engine to find as many different search engines as possible.

Check

- You can use a search engine as a source of information.

Saving and improving search results

Saving results

Once you have found information that you think will be useful, you can save the results or the individual webpage. To do this, select 'Favorites', then 'Add to Favorites' from the toolbar near the top of the screen.

Once you have selected 'Add to Favorites', a box will appear – simply select 'Add' to save the webpage.

Once you have saved a webpage you can re-open the webpage by selecting 'Favorites', then clicking on the saved page you wish to view.

Re-opening saved webpages

Search techniques

In order for the search engine to provide useful results, you need to make sure that you enter relevant information into the search box.

Information requirements

To make sure the information you find is relevant to your work you need to know that the author of the information is a 'creditable source'. This means that the author knows about the subject area and has experience in the area.

Another important factor to think about is how biased the author is likely to be. For example, has the author anything to gain by giving a bad review of a product?

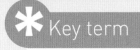

Key term

Bias
When someone's point of view influences what they say or write about something.

Activity: Saving results

Use a search engine to find the website for your school or college, then save the webpage for future reference.

Check

- You can save the results of the search for future reference.

- You can refine the search where needed to get more relevant information.

Using email to exchange information

Creating an email

Email allows you to send information to someone else (a **contact**).

To create a new email that can be sent to someone with an email address, you first need to go into the email software program, such as Microsoft Outlook®. Once you are in the program, select 'New', as shown in the screenshot below. A screen similar to the one below will appear. Select 'Mail Message' and this will take you to the screen where you can type the email that you wish to send.

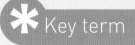
New ▾	✉ 🗋 ✗	Reply
Mail Message	Ctrl+N
Post n This Folder	Ctr+Shift+S
Folder...	Ctrl+Shift+E
Search Folder...	Ctrl+Shift+P
Navigation Pane Shortcut...	
Appointment	Ctrl+Shift+A
Meetng Request	Ctrl+Shift+Q
Contact	Ctrl+Shift+C
Distribution Lis:	Ctrl+Shift+L
Task	Ctr+Shift+K
Task Request	Ctrl+Shift+U
Journal Entry	Ctrl+Shift+J
Note	Ctrl+Shift+N
Internet Fax	Ctr+Shift+X
Choose Form...	
Outlcok Data File...	

Creating new email

Sending an email

To send an email, all you need to do is enter the email address of the person or persons that you want to send the email to into the 'To' box. You can then type your email message into the big white space provided. It is also worth putting details of the subject of the email into the 'Subject' box.

Writing an email

Activity: Sending emails

Write an email to a friend explaining what's going on in your favourite TV programme right now.

Check

- Email is a very popular way of exchanging information.

- You can send email to one or more people.

Other ways of exchanging information through IT

File attachments

You can also send **attachments** when emailing. To do this, select 'Attach'. You can then go to where the file is stored on your computer and select it. This attaches the file to the email.

Copy and paste

If the information that you want to send is not saved as a file – for example, a webpage – you can copy and paste the web address as a link into the body of the email. The person receiving the email will be able to click on to this link to view the webpage.

Attachment
A file that is attached and sent within an email.

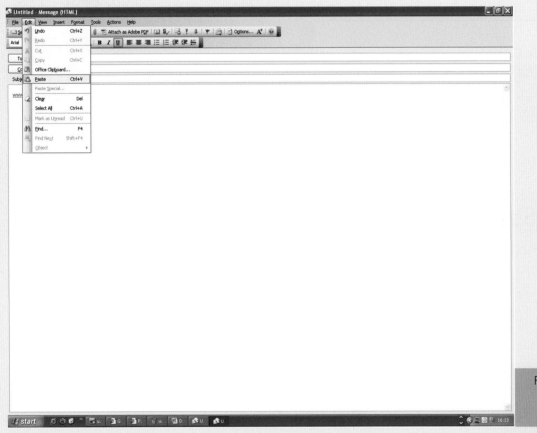

Pasting web addresses

To paste the website link into your email, click where you would like the link to appear, then select 'Paste'. To make the web address appear as a link, press 'enter' and the link should <u>appear like this</u>.

An email with website link

Activity: Sending links via email

Choose five search engines and send website links for each of them in an email.

Check

- You can copy and paste weblinks and email them.

Tools for communication

Using your address book

To help you use IT to **communicate**, it is a good idea to save all your email addresses so that they are easily accessible for future reference.

See page 72 of Unit 109 for information on how to add an email address to your **address book**.

Calendars

Email software, such as Microsoft Outlook®, also provides you with a useful calendar tool. Calendar tools allow you to plan tasks and meetings, and set reminders.

Calendar function

Tasks and to-do lists

Tasks, or a to-do list, can also be set up on email software such as Microsoft Outlook®. To set up a task, select 'Task', and then enter the details of the task in the box.

Adding tasks

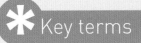

Key terms

Communication
Interaction between two or more people or devices.

Address book
A virtual book that stores details such as email addresses.

Task
A specific piece of work required to be completed, such as an assignment.

Arranging meetings

Meetings can also be arranged using email software, where you can be invited or you can invite people to attend via an email message.

To use Microsoft Outlook® to create a meeting, select 'Calendar' then 'New'. Then enter the details of the meeting (time, date, place) and select 'Invite Attendees'. Finish by clicking 'Send'.

Creating a meeting invitation

Activity: Arrange meetings via email

Invite a friend to a revision session using email software.

Check

- Email software has some very useful tools for communication, such as electronic calendars.

ASSESSMENT OVERVIEW

While working through this unit, you will have prepared for completing the following assessment tasks:

○	1.1 Use appropriate sources of IT-based and other forms of information to meet needs	Pages 26–27
○	1.2 Recognise different features of information	Pages 26–27
○	1.3 Recognise copyright constraints on the use of information	Pages 26–27
○	2.1 Access, navigate and search Internet sources of information purposefully and effectively	Pages 28–29
○	2.2 Use appropriate search techniques to locate and select relevant information	Pages 28–29
○	2.3 Indicate how the information meets requirements and is fit for purpose	Pages 30–31
○	3.1 Create, access, read and respond appropriately to email and other IT-based communication	Pages 32–33
○	3.2 Use IT tools to maintain an address book and schedule activities	Pages 36–37

edexcel

Assignment tips

- Practise using different sources to do your research. Have a look through the different sources of information listed at the beginning of this unit. Try to think of a reason why that information source is better than the others.
- Try sending emails containing links to websites that you have found useful.
- Set up a meeting using the email/calendar function to invite people to a revision session.
- Always try to understand the *quality* of the information you have found when researching, especially when using the Internet.

USING THE INTERNET

The Internet is used for almost every area of our lives. It has all kinds of information waiting to be found, and all kinds of resources to help answer any kind of question. Over 50 per cent of the UK's population is now online, and an estimated 450 million people are online around the world.

In this unit, you will:

- Learn how to connect to the Internet

- Use browser tools and learn how to navigate webpages

- Practise searching effectively online

- Use resource websites, and contribute to forums

Internet cafés around the world help people to stay in touch.

Connecting to the Internet

What is the Internet?

The Internet is many 'international' computers, connected to form one large 'network'. You could think of it as an 'International Network' ('Inter-Net').

There are many different ways to connect to the Internet. Each method has advantages and disadvantages:

	Dial up	Broadband	Mobile device (3G)
Speed	56kbps (128kbps max) Very slow!	512kbps (40mbps) Fast to very fast!	3.6mbps (7.2Mbps max) Slow to fast
Accessibility	From any landline	Broadband-ready landline	From any location with 3G signal
Reliability	Fair to good	Good	Depends on signal
Cost	From 1p per min (£10 per month contract)	Monthly cost @ £12pm (usually 5GB of data per month)	£1 per GB of data (or monthly contract)

A wireless modem used for connecting a computer to the Internet

Activity: Think

If you were in the middle of the countryside, which connection type would be most likely to get you connected to the Internet?

What do you need to access the Internet?

Internet Service Providers (ISPs)

Your **Internet Service Provider (ISP)** acts as gateway between your **hardware** and the Internet. They will give you a user name and password, and any necessary hardware (such as a modem). You might be aware of examples of ISPs such as BT, Virgin Media and TalkTalk.

Computer ⟶ modem ⟶ ISP ⟶ Internet

Modems and networks

Today, most homes connect to the Internet via a wireless modem (or wireless router). By using wi-fi (wireless connection) you can access the Internet through your wireless router. This means you can use your laptop in the garden.

Businesses and schools/colleges are more likely to use a network to connect to the Internet. Such organisations have hundreds of computers in one building. Connecting these computers together forms a large local network called a LAN (Local Area Network).

Activity: Internet connections

Make a list of the different ways of connecting to the Internet. Which way do you use?

Check

- Dial up, broadband and mobile devices are the most popular ways of accessing the Internet.

- You need an Internet Service Provider and a modem or network to access the Internet.

Key terms

Internet Service Provider (ISP)
A company that allows you to connect to the Internet.

Hardware
The physical parts of a computer that you need in order to be able to connect to the Internet.

Web browsers

Web browsers allow us to view webpages on the Internet and to travel around them, interacting with different things on the page. There are many different web browsers available: for example, Microsoft Internet Explorer®.

Browser tools

Browsers have special tools to help you view and use webpages.

✳ Key term

Web browser
Software that lets you visit websites (examples include Internet Explorer® and Firefox®).

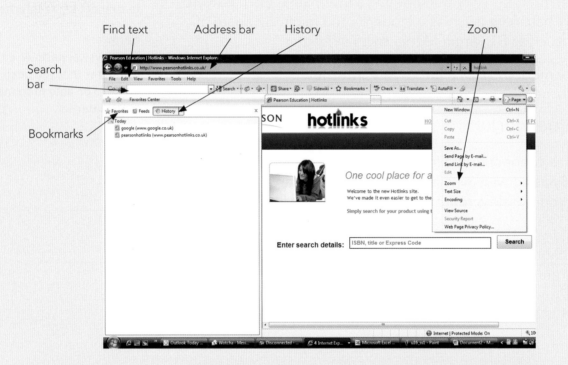

Tool	What it does
Address bar	Type in a URL (for example, www.bbc.co.uk) and the browser will take you to the right webpage.
Search bar	You can insert search terms here and the browser will find related webpages.
Bookmarks	Your browser will 'remember' those pages that you ask it to.
Zoom	You can zoom in to particular sections of the webpage.
Find text	You can search for certain words on the webpage.
History	You can save your browsing history.
Saved data	Your browsed websites can remember user names and passwords and other information if you want it to.

Activity: Think

Which browser tool would you use to remember important web addresses?

Browser settings

Settings on a browser can be changed. You can personalise your browser and customise it to help you work in a more efficient and quicker way. For example, you could:

- Change the home page of the browser

- Change the search engine you use

- Change the size of the text on each website

- Adjust the privacy settings.

Activity: Home page

Try changing the home page on your browser to your favourite search engine. This is the page that your browser will always open with. (HINT: You can do this in 'Settings'.)

✔ Check

- Your browser is the program you use to view the Internet.

- You can change your browser settings to suit your needs.

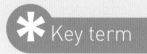
Accessibility

Some people have special needs when using a computer. This might be problems with their vision, or hearing difficulties, for example.

'**Accessibility**' means helping people with difficulties use a computer more easily. To help them we could:

- Increase font size to make reading webpages easier

- Design websites that make navigation very easy: for example, by using large browser buttons

- Use different colours and zoom areas to make things easier to see

- Use screen readers, where software reads the content of webpages back to the user

- Increase the volume for people with hearing difficulties.

Help facilities

If you are having difficulties with anything on your computer you can use the help function in the web browser. This is true whether you have special accessibility needs or not.

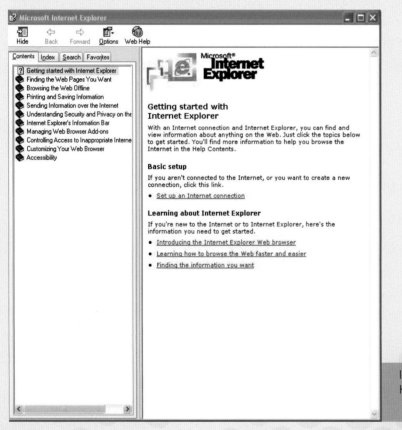

Internet Explorer® (Windows) Help

* Key term

Accessibility
Helping people with difficulties use a computer more easily.

*** Functional skills

Learning about accessibility and what it means will help improve your skills in English.

To find the help function: press F1 on your keyboard or use the help icon.

You can also use search engines by typing in your question. There are plenty of other people who will be able to share your problems, and even offer answers.

Activity: Imagine

Imagine that you have very limited sight – think about how you would visit and use your favourite website.

What could that website do to help you?

Check

- Some people have special needs when using a computer, such as limited sight or hearing.

- Even if you don't have special needs, you still might need help. You can search for help on your computer and on the Internet.

Search engines

Whatever question you might have, whatever topic you are interested in, whatever picture you want to see, almost everything is available online … but how do you find it?

Search engines have revolutionised how we use the Internet. A search engine will give you a list of websites that they think match what you are looking for. These are the **search results**.

Before you choose from your search results, scan the title and brief description. Not all webpages are useful, and some may not even contain the information you searched for. Visually check: the top search result is not always the best or most trustworthy.

✳ Key term

Search results
Results (websites) that are found by a search engine when you type in your search text.

Search results on Google search engine

◎ Activity: Your favourite search engines

Visit your favourite search engine and search for something that interests you. Did the information you expected come out at the top?

📁 Case study:
Bias

Charlie is a Manchester United fan. He writes a match report about a Manchester United versus Brighton match. This is for a Manchester United fan website that he runs himself. His team lose, Brighton winning by one goal after a last-minute penalty.

Activity: Group discussion

How do you think Charlie will write the report?

- Fairly – with a balanced report on both sides?

- More on Manchester United's side (i.e. biased towards Manchester United)?

- More on Brighton's side (biased towards Brighton)?

Searching tips

When typing your search query into a search engine, the more specific you are, the better the results will be.

For example: if you type in 'football', you will find a search engine return around 333,000,000 (million) webpages! To narrow down your search, and improve your results, you could type in 'football + soccer', or 'football + Man Utd'.

This would find webpages that are about 'football', (+) your second search criteria. You can also use the minus sign (-): for example, 'football - American' to find webpages about football minus your second search criteria.

Activity: Search queries

Try a search query for 'football', and use the plus (+) and minus (-) signs when searching for your favourite football team. You could also try this with other search criteria, for example, 'bands'.

✓ Check

- You should always check information you find on the Internet for validity and bias.

- You can make your searches better by using the plus (+) and minus (-) technique.

Functional skills

Knowing about bias will help improve your language skills in **English**.

! Remember

You can reference where you found a piece of information. This is bookmarking and allows you to return to it later.

✳ Key terms

Search query/criteria
The text you type into a search engine to find webpages.

Bias
When someone's point of view influences what they say or write about something.

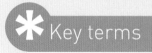
Communicating online

The World Wide Web is all about communication.

Type of communication	Activity
Sharing information	Posting links to webpages on social networking sites; emailing links; visiting chatrooms.
Reading information	Visiting and reading webpages.
Watching information	Podcasts, YouTube.
Publishing information	Creating your own webpage, blog, or social network.

Which of the above forms of communication have you used on the Web this week?

Activity: Blogging

- Visit a search engine, and search for 'setting up my own blog'.

- Now spend 15 minutes creating your own blog site. It's very easy and fun.

Submitting information online

Submitting information online is very easy. Usually this is done through a 'form' on a webpage.

You can also interact with websites through recommendations, ratings, reviews, forums and wikis.

Wikis are where users add content to a webpage. The idea is that many minds are better than one, so if many people contribute to a 'wiki', then it should have really interesting and accurate content. However, there are downsides to lots of people being involved, such as too much information, the accuracy of the information, bias, etc.

Submitting information online

Remember

You can download and save information from webpages (for example, by cutting and pasting text into your own files, or saving images).

Activity: Group discussion

What are the possible dangers of having many people contribute to a webpage (wikis)?

Check

- You can share, read, watch and publish information on the Web.

- You can be really creative in how you do this with blogs and other new web forms of communication.

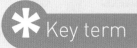
Safety and security

Threats to users

You can be exposed to all sorts of potential threats on the Internet. Knowing about these is essential to protecting yourself from them.

Speaking with unknown individuals on the Internet can be dangerous. People may use false identities to get to younger Internet users. This is sometimes called 'grooming'.

! Remember

You should take steps to protect yourself:

- Only chat to known friends.
- Don't add just anyone to your 'friends' list.
- Do your research about who wants to be your friend.
- Never agree to meet anyone from the Internet if you don't personally know them.
- Keep your personal information safe and secure.

Some sites have a button you can press to report online abuse

◎ Activity: Think

How secure is your personal information on your social networking page? Can anyone see your personal information, such as your mobile number or email address?

Cyber-bullying

Bullying is an unpleasant experience. With the ease of publishing information, and sharing this information with the world, cyber-bullying has become a huge problem among Internet users.

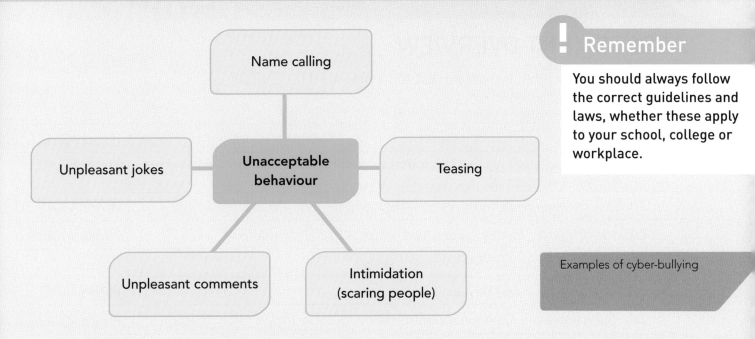

! **Remember**

You should always follow the correct guidelines and laws, whether these apply to your school, college or workplace.

Examples of cyber-bullying

How to minimise risks

You can report inappropriate behaviour to your tutor, or to your friends and family. It's important to do so, not just to protect yourself, but to help protect others who may not be so Internet-safe.

As well as keeping yourself safe online, you should use the correct software to protect your computer from viruses, Trojans, spyware and adware. These are all programs that can get onto your computer when you download files. They can cause a lot of damage, or spy on you and steal personal information.

Activity: Group discussion

What would you do if you:

- Were being threatened in any way online

- Had a virus on your computer?

✔ Check

- Grooming and cyber-bullying are serious issues that should always be reported.

- You can protect yourself on the Internet by guarding your personal information properly.

ASSESSMENT OVERVIEW

While working through this unit, you will have prepared for completing the following tasks:

○	1.1 Access the Internet or intranet	Pages 42–43
○	1.2 Identify different types of connection methods that can be used to access the Internet	Pages 42–43
○	2.1 Use browser tools to navigate webpages	Pages 44–45
○	2.2 Identify when to change browser settings to aid navigation	Pages 44–45
○	2.3 Adjust browser settings to meet needs	Page 45
○	2.4 Use browser help facilities	Pages 46–47
○	3.1 Select and use appropriate search techniques to locate information	Pages 48–49
○	3.3 Use references to make it easier to find information another time	Page 49
○	3.4 Download and save different types of information from the Internet	Page 54
○	4.1 Select and use tools and techniques to communicate information online	Pages 50–51
○	4.2 Use browser tools to share information sources with others	Page 50
○	4.3 Submit information online using forms or interactive sites	Pages 50–51
○	4.4 Identify opportunities to post or publish material to websites	Pages 50–51
○	5.1 Identify the threats to user safety when working online	Pages 52–53
○	5.2 Outline how to minimise Internet security risks	Pages 52–53
○	5.3 Work responsibly and take appropriate safety and security precautions when working online	Pages 52–53
○	5.4 Keep personal information secure	Pages 52–53
○	5.5 Follow relevant laws, guidelines and procedures for the use of the Internet	Page 53

edexcel

Assignment tips

- The faster the Internet connection speed, the faster you are able to download from the Internet.
- Browsers can be customised to help you browse the Internet quicker and in the way you want.
- Always use the Help facilities available. F1 is a shortcut key to the Help Menu.
- When using a search engine, be specific with your search query, and use the + and - keys.
- Don't forget to bookmark your favourite websites. Finding them later will be much quicker and easier.
- When communicating online, don't give your personal information away. Keep this safe and secure.

It is likely that you already own and use a mobile phone for texting, making telephone calls and taking photos. However, many mobile devices available today are capable of doing much more.

Mobile devices are playing an increasingly large role in day-to-day business. This unit will provide you with an insight into the professional capabilities of mobile devices.

Mobile devices are not only phones – they can be personal digital assistants (PDAs), portable media players and electronic organisers.

In this unit you will learn to:

- Set up a mobile device
- Transfer data
- Use applications and files
- Keep the device working well

Is this more than just a mobile phone?

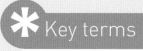

Setting up devices

Basic set up

When setting up a new mobile device, it is good practice to fully charge the battery before using the device.

Most mobile devices allow you to:

- access the Internet
- view emails
- maintain diary or calendar features.

Sim cards

To use most mobile devices, you will need a sim card. This is inserted into the mobile device before being used.

Do you know how to remove a sim card?

Features of mobile devices

The display

The mobile device will have a menu screen which will show a list of options available, such as contacts, messaging, calendar, Internet.

Contacts	
Messaging	
Calls	
Calendar	
Internet	

Some of the main options usually found on the menu screen have icons such as these.

Device settings

If you have ever looked at the settings menu on a mobile device, you will have noticed that settings can be changed for a number of events.

Setting	What it does
Screen resolution	Screen picture resolution (quality) can be altered. The higher the setting, the quicker the battery power will be used up.
Mute	You can turn the sound off completely.
Volume	Volume can be adjusted to be louder or quieter.
Ringtone	Mobile devices usually come with a range of standard ringtones built in. Alternatively, you can select your favourite song as your ringtone.
Themes	Most mobile devices come with a variety of themes that can be used to personalise it.

! Remember

If mobile devices are going to be used in organisations, then your employer might ask you to use certain security measures to protect company information.

Activity: Change your ringtone

Change the ringtone on your phone to another tone. Remember not to disturb anyone else and always ask your tutor first.

Check

- You can change the settings on a mobile device to meet your needs and preferences.

Use of applications and files

Applications and files

Mobile devices come with a range of applications that enable you to store, manage and access different types of information. Some of the most popular applications are:

- Address book: a list of all your friends' details, such as telephone numbers and addresses.

- Calendar: a list of the dates from the calendar year. Events for each date can be added.

- Media manager: an area on a phone where you can control media files, such as music and videos.

- Browser: an application on your phone to view the Internet.

- Games: some devices come with free games, and you can often download more.

- Notes: an area on the phone to record comments and reminders.

- Messages: almost every phone allows the user to send a text message to another phone.

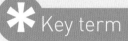

Key term

Stylus
A small pen-shaped instrument used with a computer screen.

Activity: Add to a calendar

Add your birthday to the calendar on your mobile device.

Data input

Information and files can be added to mobile devices in a number of ways: for example, many of the popular smart phones available today, including the Apple iPhone, have a touchscreen instead of buttons. This allows you to use your fingers to type information into the device, make calls, etc.

Other devices have touchscreens, but they need to be used with a **stylus** instead of fingers.

A stylus

Keyboards can also be found on some mobile devices, usually in those that do not have a touchscreen, such as a BlackBerry.

A BlackBerry keyboard

Some mobile devices offer voice command, where the device will respond to spoken commands through the use of voice control.

Activity: Explore the menu

Explore your mobile phone and comment on the menu system within your phone. Is it easy to use?

✓ Check

- Most mobile devices have many different and interesting applications. Today, most can now be used as much more than just a phone.

Transferring data

Sharing information

Devices can be connected to share information. To do this you should use a **secure connection**. Here are some ways to do this:

- Password control: set a password on your device. This reduces the risk of unwanted connections from unknown devices.

- Bluetooth®: can be used to transfer and receive data over short distances using radio waves.

- Infrared: can be used to transfer and receive data over short distances using light.

- Cable: you can connect to devices using the traditional method of cabling. The two devices are physically connected.

- **Synchronisation** software: some devices come with software which allows connections to be made between similar devices.

Transferring information

Information can be transferred from a mobile device to a computer or vice versa using a USB cable. This attaches the mobile device to the computer.

A USB can be plugged into the computer using sockets as pictured here.

> **!** **Remember**
>
> - Protect your personal information.
> - The person you are talking to may be using a fake picture – be careful.
> - Always use appropriate language when communicating via the Internet.

Synchronisation is where two devices talk to each other to ensure both are sending and receiving the correct information at the correct time and in the correct order. The two separate devices will also ensure that the most current file is used and not deleted.

Staying safe

When connecting to the Internet, regardless of which device you use, it is very important you take steps to stay safe.

> ◎ **Activity: Personal data**
>
> Think of an item of personal data that you might need to protect, e.g. personal information on your mobile phone. Why is it important to do this? Think of some ways you can protect this information.

> ✓ **Check**
>
> - Many different devices can be connected to each other using various technologies.
>
> - Online security is extremely important and you should be careful at all times.

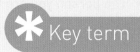
Maintaining performance

Some devices can be very expensive and cost a lot to replace. It is vital that equipment is well looked after. You can do this by carrying out the following **maintenance** tips:

- Charge the battery only when the device's battery is completely drained.

- Clean the handset – this should be done with a special dry cloth.

- Turn applications off when not in use.

- Turn off Bluetooth® and other connection media when not in use.

Protecting your battery

- Set Bluetooth® to off when you are not using it.

- Always let the battery go flat before charging it.

- Turn off any animated screensavers.

- Turn off the vibrate notification function.

> **✱ Key term**
>
> **Maintenance**
> Cleaning, checking, improving, modifying to ensure something continues to work properly.

Why is it important to let the battery go flat before charging it?

Activity: Guidance poster

Produce a guidance poster on maintaining your mobile device. You could include information on how to make the battery last longer.

Device problems

Many of us rely on our mobile devices to keep in touch when we are on the move, so when they go wrong it can be very frustrating.

First of all, look at the troubleshooting section of the manufacturer's guidelines, which provides practical tips to resolve common problems. You might also be able to identify and resolve the problem by searching online. Below are a few basic tips to try and solve minor problems:

- Lack of signal: move closer to a window and remove any potential barriers between the phone and the mast.

- Can't receive messages: it could be as simple as the sim card is full. If so, you will have to remove some information in order to receive more.

- Can't connect to the network: is Bluetooth® or your wi-fi turned on? If not turn them on and try again.

If none of this works, then you will need seek expert advice.

Remember

Each manufacturer will have guidelines on their products to help you. These should come free of charge with the product.

Key term

Advice
Information from someone who has greater knowledge about something.

Activity: Troubleshooting

Read the troubleshooting section of the manufacturer's guidelines for your mobile device. This will help you learn about common problems that might occur.

Check

- Keeping applications running unnecessarily on your mobile device can reduce its battery life.

- Looking through the manufacturer's guidelines can help you learn how to deal with problems with your mobile device.

ASSESSMENT OVERVIEW

While working through this unit, you will have prepared for completing
the following assessment tasks:

○	1.1	Set up the mobile device for use	Pages 56–57
○	1.2	Use mobile device interface features effectively	Pages 56–57
○	1.3	Identify when and how to adjust device settings	Pages 56–57
○	1.4	Adjust device settings to meet needs	Pages 56–57
○	1.5	Identify any specific health and safety issues associated with the use of mobile devices	Pages 56–57
○	1.6	Follow guidelines and procedures for the use of mobile devices	Pages 56–57
○	2.1	Identify the different applications on the mobile device and what they can be used for	Pages 58–59
○	2.2	Select and use applications and files on the mobile device for an appropriate purpose	Pages 58–59
○	2.3	Input data accurately into a mobile device	Pages 58–59
○	2.4	Organise, store and retrieve data on a mobile device	Pages 58–59
○	3.1	Identify different types of secure connection methods that can be used between devices	Pages 60–61
○	3.2	Transfer information to and from the mobile device	Pages 60–61
○	3.3	Recognise copyright and other constraints on the use and transfer of information	Pages 60–61
○	3.4	Identify why it is important to stay safe, keep information secure and to respect others when using a mobile device	Pages 60–61
○	3.5	Keep information secure when using a mobile device	Pages 60–61
○	4.1	Identify factors that can affect performance of the mobile device	Pages 62–63
○	4.2	Use appropriate techniques to maintain the performance of the mobile device	Pages 62–63
○	4.3	Identify common problems that occur with mobile devices and what causes them	Pages 62–63
○	4.4	Identify when to try to solve a problem and where to get expert advice	Pages 62–63
○	4.5	Use available resources to respond quickly and appropriately to common device problems	Pages 62–63

edexcel

Assignment tips

- Ensure that you understand what is needed in order to set up a mobile device.
- Practise using applications on your mobile devices. You should focus on applications such as the calendar and address book.
- Research different connection techniques.
- Practise performing security checks on your mobile device.

Email is an electronic handwritten letter. It is a quick and effective way of communicating with people.

Many businesses have adopted email as their main way of communicating with their customers.

There are estimated to be around 250 billion emails being sent every day.

Emails can contain so much more than just text. You can include 'attachments', which might include things like pictures, sounds and documents.

In this unit, you will learn to:

- Create and send emails, including sending attachments

- Stay safe and respect others when using email

- Create an address book to store email addresses

- Reply to email and respond appropriately

- Organise your emails into folders, and delete unwanted emails

- Deal with common email problems

Can you guess how many emails are sent around the world every day?

Email

Email software

There are many different types of software used to write (**compose**) emails. The most common is Microsoft Outlook®, which is software that runs on your computer.

Web-based email software, such as Hotmail, Gmail and YahooMail, do not use software on your computer, they run on the Internet instead.

It doesn't matter which way you use email, the same rules are applied when you want to write an email.

You need an address to send 'To'.

You need to include a 'Subject' to give a brief introduction into what the email is about.

You need to write your message in the large box.

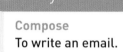

Key term

Compose
To write an email.

Using email in Microsoft Outlook®

Formatting

When writing your message, you have many '**formatting**' options. These will include:

- Changing the font type

- Changing the colour

- Adding bullet or number lists

- Aligning the text.

Key term

Formatting
The way information is presented.

Other email options

The 'CC' ('Carbon Copy') field allows you to send the same message to more than one person.

The 'BCC' ('Blind Carbon Copy') field allows you to send the same message to more than one person, without anyone knowing that you did this.

The 'Reply' button is a quick way to reply to an email. It will automatically start a new message, and include the sender's address in the 'To' field.

Activity: Sending email messages

Using your personal email:

1. 'Compose' a new message.

2. In the address field, type in a classmate's address.

3. In the address 'CC' field, type in a different classmate's address.

4. Type 'ICT' in the subject line.

5. In the message 'body', type: 'Please reply to confirm you have received this email'.

6. Send the email, and wait for each classmate to reply.

Activity: Writing an email

Write an email to a company to find out if they have any jobs that you could apply for.

Check

- Email is a very fast method of communication, and is very effective.

- You can send an email to more than one person.

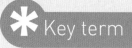

Attaching files and sending emails

When writing emails, you will also have an option to insert 'attachments'. Attachments are files that are located on your computer that you may wish to send to someone. You are simply 'attaching' the files to your message.

The file size of the attachment (how big it is) needs to be considered here. If the attachment is too large, it will not be able to send. Think of a poor postman trying to carry a parcel that weighs as much as a car.

✳ Key term

Attachment
A file that is attached and sent within an email.

Activity: Email attachments

Imagine you work for an estate agent, and you are about to send an email to a customer. What might you attach in that email?

- Photos of properties

- Layouts and diagrams of properties

- A map of how to get to there.

Sending an email

When you have composed your message and it is ready to send, you should spell check the message in case you have made any spelling mistakes. Typing errors are common, and you don't want to look unprofessional.

Netiquette is also important. You need to check if your email is meant to be professional, or if you are sending it to friends or family.

Finally you should also check the address. If the address is incorrect, it will not reach its destination.

boss@myworkplace.com is different to bass@myworkplace.com. If the address is incorrect, the message could end up somewhere in the digital abyss!

When you click the 'Send' button, the email is instantly sent, and within moments it will reach its destination.

Key term

Netiquette
Rules for how to write in emails and on the Internet.

Functional skills

Learning to check your email messages, and correct any mistakes will improve your skills in English.

Activity: Email functions

- Can you think of any benefits of sending the same message to more than one person (using the 'CC' field)?

- What are the advantages of replying to a message you have been sent, rather than composing a new blank message?

Summary

- You can include attachments in emails, such as pictures, sounds and other files.

- You can format emails by changing fonts, sizes and colours.

Staying safe

Anyone can send you an email, and sometimes they may contain a **virus**. Viruses are sometimes found within attachments, so you must be sure that you trust the sender of the email before opening any attachments.

You should treat emails with **caution**, and be wary of the sender's intentions.

✳ Key terms

Virus
A file that can cause disruption and harm to your computer.

Caution
Taking care when reading and replying to emails.

Activity: Keeping your computer safe

- Can you think of what damage could be caused by a computer being infected with a virus?

- Emails are an easy route into your computer. How could you help protect your computer?

Respect others

Emails are a quick and easy way to communicate with people. However, we must be cautious and show care when writing emails.

Work hours - Message

File Edit View Insert Format Tools Table Window Help

To... boss@myworkplace.com
Cc...
Subject: Work hours

Arial 10

Dear Sir

I am writing a short email to request time off for personal reasons.

I have completed all my set tasks for today and would be very grateful if I could leave early to attend personal matters.

Thank you for this consideration and I look forward to hearing from you.

Kindest regards,

Employee

Do you think this is appropriate language to use when writing to your boss?

70

You should demonstrate respect when writing or replying to an email. Language is important. The way you write your email is important and you should think how the person reading it will feel.

You wouldn't use 'text speak' when writing an email to your boss, though you may be a little more relaxed with your language when writing to your family or friends.

Functional skills

Learning to think about how you have written your message, and whether it is appropriate for the audience, will improve your skills in English.

Activity: Spelling in emails

Can you think of any way to check the spelling of your emails? For example, by re-reading your email carefully.

Confidentiality

Confidentiality is important.

Emails can be sent to many people at once. Information within emails may be personal, and sometimes sensitive, which you do not want to share with everyone.

Take care when adding an address in the 'To' field. It is very easy to add more than one address and nothing can be changed once your email is sent.

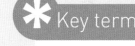

Key term

Confidentiality
Keeping personal and private information safe.

Check

- Emails can contain viruses. Be sure that you trust the person who has sent you an email before reading it.

- Emails are private, but can also be sent to a number of people. Be sure of who you are sending it to, and that the email is intended for them.

- You should check your language is suitable for the person you are sending the email to.

Address books

An **address book** is a very useful tool. Email addresses are often very long, and complicated to remember. How do you remember whose email is funkydancemaster62@hotmail.com, for example ... ?

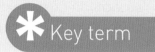

✱ Key term

Address book
A virtual book that stores details such as email addresses.

Using an address book in Microsoft Outlook®

It is difficult to remember an email address, and even harder to make sure you have spelt it correctly. Was it a .com or .co.uk at the end, or was it a .org? An address book will store all of this information for you. This means you only have to enter someone's email address once, and the computer will remember it for you. So the next time you want to email your friend, you can find them in your address book and, more importantly, find their email address quickly and easily.

◎ Activity: Email addresses

Think of those of your friends who have an email address. Can you remember their full addresses correctly?

Distribution lists

You can create a **distribution list** from your address book. A distribution list is simply a list of email addresses from your address book that you have grouped together. For example, you can group all of your family members' email addresses, and create a distribution list called 'family'. You can then create a single email and send it to your whole family at once, without entering each email address separately.

Businesses might create a distribution list of customers' email addresses in order to send an email telling them about a new product or service.

The benefits of having an address book include:

- All email addresses are stored

- You can locate an email address by 'searching' the address book

- You can delete and edit entries in your address book

- You can create distribution lists, which allow you to send an email to many people at the same time

- Address books can contain other information, such as birthdays, addresses, and telephone numbers.

✳ Key term

Distribution list
Similar to an address book, but with pre-selected entries within the address book so that you can quickly and easily send the same email to everyone within the list.

Activity: Why use an address book?

Time how long it takes you to write down three of your friends' email addresses. Which do you think is quicker – finding an email address from an address book or trying to remember them?

✔ Check

- An address book is a virtual book that stores details such as email addresses.

- A distribution list is a list of email addresses from your address book that you have grouped together.

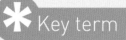
Responding to emails

Usually when you receive an email, you will need to **respond** to it. Your reply to that email forms part of an 'email communication' – perhaps a customer asking a question, or friends wanting to know what you are doing over the weekend. The netiquette you will use in writing your email depends on who sent the email.

Professional emails

In business, it is expected that a written response will contain:

● Professional language (for example, 'Dear Sir' and 'Yours sincerely')

● Courteous manner (for example, 'Your email is important to us, and we will respond as soon as possible')

● Your name and title (for example, 'Mathew Brown – Head of Department').

Activity: Professional emails

● Why do you think it is important to ensure that emails to customers follow the three bullet points above?

● How would customers feel if your emails were not professional?

Organisations that send regular emails will have guidelines and **procedures** that employees must use. This might include words that they must not use in an email: for example, 'Cheers', 'Ta', 'C U L8tr'. Such guidelines and procedures are usually designed to make sure that any emails sent are professional and reflect the attitudes of the company – not those of the employee writing them.

Employees are also trained on how to respond and reply to emails. As well as using their organisation's guidelines and policies, employees will also need to identify important emails, and decide which emails are answered first.

Activity: Dealing with emails

Two emails arrive in your inbox at the same time. One is from a customer who is angry, and the other is from your boss. Which email do you respond to first?

Saving your messages

Important emails should also be saved in case you need to re-read them later. Whatever email program you use, you will have the ability to create folders to store your messages. Some email accounts have the ability to search your entire inbox to help find emails.

When you are composing your email, you can save a 'draft copy' of it, and return to it later. This works just like creating a Word document and saving it in order to continue working on it the next day.

Unwanted emails are a nuisance. How do you find out if an email is worth deleting? You will need to read the email, and decide if you should delete it, or if you need to reply to it.

Activity: Spam filters

Go into your personal email, and look for a 'Spam' or 'Junk' folder. See how many 'junk/spam' emails are filtered by your email spam filter. If you didn't have this 'filter', all of those spam emails would arrive in your inbox!

Check

- When you receive an email, you will usually need to respond to it.

- You need to use different writing rules and styles for different situations: for example, in business you will need to use a more formal writing style.

Common email problems

There are many problems that can occur when sending emails. For instance, if you try to send an email with an attachment, you may be restricted by the number of attachments you can include in one email. Trying to attach too many files may result in an email not sending.

File size is another possible problem when sending emails. Generally you will not be able to send emails that are larger than 5MB.

Other common problems include:

- Wrong email address
- No Internet connection
- Email server not working.

Viruses can be hidden within attachments, so be sure that you scan attachments with anti-virus software before you open them.

A very large file size may cause problems for the sender and/ or for the recipient

Activity: Email viruses

How would you react if you thought an email contained a virus?

Spam

Spam is a big problem with email. Spam is essentially unwanted email.

Spam emails are usually emails that are trying to sell you something. They are usually sent from an unknown sender. This makes it very difficult to stop spam arriving in your inbox.

Spam filters try to block emails, but the danger is that 'real' emails can mistakenly be blocked too.

Phishing

Phishing emails are emails that try to trick you into giving your passwords or private information.

eBay is a huge target for phishing scams. Fake emails are sent that pretend to be from eBay, requesting users to change their password, or re-directing users to fake sites. People are tricked into giving out their passwords and criminals then use this information to steal money or access bank accounts.

Activity: Group discussion

If you received an email asking you to confirm your online bank account by replying with your password, would you go along with it?

✔ Check

- There are several common email-related problems that can occur, such as phishing and spam.
- You need to be alert and on your guard when dealing with emails.

✳ Key terms

Spam
Unwanted emails, often trying to sell something.

Phishing
A scam email designed to trick you into giving passwords and account details.

Functional skills

Learning to read emails thoroughly and judging if an email is genuine will help improve your skills in English.

! Remember

It is very easy to follow instructions contained in an email. Treat emails as you would treat complete strangers ... with caution.

ASSESSMENT OVERVIEW

While working through this unit, you will have prepared for completing the following assessment tasks:

○	1.1 Use software tools to compose and format email messages	Pages 66–67
○	1.2 Attach files to email messages	Page 68
○	1.3 Send email messages	Page 69
○	2.1 Identify how to stay safe and respect others when using email	Pages 70–71
○	3.1 Use an address book to store and retrieve contact information	Pages 72–73
○	4.1 Follow guidelines and procedures for using email	Pages 74–75
○	4.2 Identify when and how to respond to email messages	Pages 74–75
○	4.3 Read and respond to email messages appropriately	Pages 74–75
○	5.1 Identify what messages to delete and when to do so	Pages 74–75
○	5.2 Organise and store email messages	Pages 74–75
○	6.1 Respond appropriately to common email problems	Pages 76–77

edexcel

Assignment tips

- Emails from people you don't know should always be treated with caution.
- Attachments should always be scanned with anti-virus software before you open them.
- Never give your passwords or personal information to anyone requesting them via email.
- When you write an email, double-check it before you send it. Mistakes are easily made, and there is no 'undo' button once it has been sent.
- Create a back-up of your address book.

IT SOFTWARE FUNDAMENTALS

Software can be used for many different tasks. There are many different types of software available to the user.

Software can be described as the applications that run on your computer. They allow you to interact with the computer hardware (the physical elements of a computer).

With so many software options available, it is very important that as a computer user you make the correct choice.

In this unit, you will learn to:

- Use the right software for the task

- Use correct formatting techniques to enhance information

- Present information in a way that suits the audience

- Use IT tools to present information

When might you use presentation software?

Software applications

As computer users, we use many different types of software. We also use computers for many different types of tasks. It is essential that we use the correct software for the correct task. Below are some examples of software and their uses:

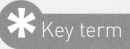

Software	Use
Word processing	To create formal documents, such as letters and reports.
Spreadsheets	To store financial and numerical information. You can also carry out calculations with spreadsheets.
Databases	To store large amount of data. A typical example could be a collection of learner details.
Presentations	Normally used to show information in a professional manner.
Graphics	Normally used to create pictures. An example could be a logo.
Internet browser	To look at websites.
Email	To send electronic information to another person.
Audio	To listen to and store music files.
Video	To watch and store video files.

Activity: Identify software types

As you can see from the list above, there are many different types of software available. List all the types of software you would use on an average session on Facebook.

Types of information

There are many different types of information. You can use the following types of information in the appropriate situation:

- Text: typed information, can be letters and numbers

- Numbers: information that can used in calculations

- Images: images can be used to explain a complex situation

- Sound: to enhance a presentation

- Graphics: used to create a logo

- Data records: the information within a database.

Case study:
Fliers

Jennifer works at a leisure centre. She has been asked to use the staff computer to produce a flier to be handed out at the centre. It has to include images of activities taking place at the centre and details of starting and finishing times for all the main classes.

Activity: Think

If you were Jennifer, what software would you use to make the flier?

Check

- There are many different types of software applications.

- It is very important to select the correct software type for the right task.

Organising information

When producing reports and other information involving text and data, you need to make sure your audience can read and clearly understand the contents of your information. There are several things you can do to ensure that your work is organised in a professional manner.

Key term

Heading
A term used to describe the subject you are writing about.

Why is it important to keep both your computer files and desk organised?

Headings

A heading is normally at the beginning of a new topic. So whenever you change the topic you should try to include a new heading. You may notice that each different topic in this book has a heading. A heading should be clear and relate to the information below. You should aim to make the heading stand out, perhaps by using the **bold** tool.

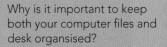

Functional skills

Organising data can help you improve your skills in English.

Lists

A list is a quick and easy way of organising several items of short pieces of text. For example, you can create a shopping list.

Activity: Lessons of the week

Produce a list of your lessons this week.

Tables

When you have several pieces of data that are closely linked to a few topics you can organise data into tables. A good example of storing data in a table could be a sports league table. Can you think of any other pieces of information that can be organised into a table?

Templates

If you repeatedly use the same information, but only slightly change certain sections, you can use a template. A template can save a lot of time. A prime example could be a template for your assignments.

Sort

At times, you can have a lot of information that can be stored in both lists and tables, but, because of the amount of data involved, it could still be hard to organise the information. A solution could be to sort the information in a certain order. The most popular sorting method is alphabetically.

Graphs and charts

Another way of organising a large amount of complex data could be to place the information into a graph. An example could be a graph to show the amount of muffins sold in a bakery for each day of the week.

When may you need to use a graph in your work?

◎ Activity: Using tables

Make a table to show your assignments in one column and your result in the column next to it.

✓ Check

- There are many different types of software applications.

- It is very important to select the correct software type for the right task.

83

Formatting different types of information

You have seen from the previous topic that you can organise information by using different techniques. You are now going to explore how to make different types of information more interesting for your audience. You will look at improving the format of **text**, **numbers** and images.

Layout

Bullets and numbering

You can make a list look more effective by assigning each list item a bullet point or a number. For example:

- computer
- screen
- desk.

Alignment

You can change the layout of text by making the edges of the text line up with each other. You can find the alignment options in the formatting toolbar.

Line spacing

When you are dealing with a large amount of text, you may wish to alter the amount of space between each line of text.

Text

The sections above have dealt with the layout of the text, but now we will focus on the text itself.

Colour

You can change the colour of the text. A good usage of colour change would be to highlight a dangerous situation in **red**.

Font

You can change the size and style of the text. Be careful not to make text too small or too big, and make sure the style is still readable.

Key terms

Text
Any letter, number or character. Or a combination of all three.

Number
A value between 0 and 9. A number can be any size.

Formatting
The way information is presented.

Numbers

Currency

When using numbers to display money, you can add the currency value to the number: for example, £1.99. Symbols such as this are usually found on the 2nd row of your computer keyboard. You normally need to press shift and the key to use them.

Percentages

When using numbers to display percentage values you should add the '%' sign to the end of the number: for example: 89%.

Decimal places

Decimal places are used to show a 'chunk' of a whole number. For example, you may write that the building was 2.7 metres tall.

Images

Size

Sometimes original sizes can be too big or too small. Therefore it is important to make sure that you use the correct size for your image.

Position

You can also place an image in different positions within the page to ensure maximum effect.

Functional skills

Practising changing number formats will help you develop your skills in Mathematics.

Activity: Using formatting techniques

Try at least one formatting technique from the lists above. You should include a technique from each of text, numbers and images sections.

Check

- You can format text, numbers and images to maximise their effect.
- Remember to use the correct formatting technique for the correct occasion.

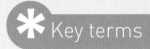
Page layout

You are now going to explore the different techniques you can apply to an entire page.

Page size

Most of the time you would be working on the same size paper, but on odd occasions you may need to use a different size.

Most types of software allow us to change the page size. The standard size is normally A4. However, you can make changes to the size to fit your needs. Can you think of any occasions when you may need to use a smaller-sized page?

Page orientation

As with page size, you may wish to change the 'shape' (orientation) of the page. This will mean altering the positioning of the page. You have two options:

- **Portrait**
- **Landscape**.

Selecting page orientation

The portrait setting is the most common setting and should be used for formal documents like letters. The landscape setting can be used to accommodate wider images that are required for the page.

Page margins

You can adjust the margins to leave more or less space between the edges of the text and the edges of the page.

Page numbering

On occasions you may need to work with multiple pages, and this may become confusing for the reader. If you have many pages in a document, you can add page numbers on each page to give them each a separate identity.

Date and time

You may have several working copies of each document. Again this may become confusing for the reader. If you put the date and time on each copy, you can keep track of when each of the versions of the document was created.

Key term

Margin
The area between the text and the edge of the page.

Activity: Adding page features

Enter the page numbers, along with the date and time, into one of your previously created documents.

Check

- You can alter the page layout of most documents.

- Extra features, such as page numbers and the date, can help improve the communication between you and your audience.

Presenting information

How you format documents and set up pages is very important. Equally important is the **presentation** of the information and checking for **accuracy**.

Accuracy

Most software applications have tools available to ensure the accuracy of your documents. Tools commonly available include:

- Spell checker: you can use the spell checker to ensure that your spelling is correct

- Grammar: you can also check to see if you are using the correct language structure within your document

- Print preview: you can use the print preview tool to ensure that the overall appearance of your document is correct.

Choosing your document

It is important to use the correct kind of document to suit the occasion.

Type of document	Use
Letter	Formal document that is used for important information.
Memo	An informal document that can be used to highlight short pieces of information.
Report	Longer document that will go into detail about the topic.
Newsletter	Short text to highlight current issues.
Poster	Short and sharp information, usually displayed in a graphical format.
Information sheet	Information placed on a factsheet.
Webpage	Used to post information on the Internet.
Multimedia presentation	Used to present information in different ways (for example, a PowerPoint file).
Budget	A financial document to show how much money is available for a project.
Invoice	A professional document used to let a company know how much to pay you.
Stock list	A list of a company's goods.

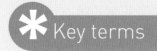
Key terms

Presentation
The appearance of an object.

Accuracy
The level of how closely something matches its required state.

Remember

Spell check all of your work.

What software could you use for each of the documents listed in the table opposite?

Activity: Create a document

Choose one of the document types in the table opposite. Make a document in this style on a topic that interests you.

Check

- It is important to check all of your work.

- You can create many different types of document, both formal and informal.

ASSESSMENT OVERVIEW

While working through this unit, you will have prepared for completing
the following assessment tasks:

○	1.1	Identify different software applications and give examples of their use	Pages 80–81
○	1.2	Select and use appropriate software applications to develop, produce and present different types of information to meet needs and solve problems	Pages 80–81
○	1.3	Identify what types of information are needed	Pages 80–81
○	2.1	Enter, organise and format different types of information to meet needs	Pages 82–83
○	2.2	Apply editing techniques to refine information as required	Pages 84–85
○	2.3	Combine information of different forms or from different sources to meet needs	Pages 84–85
○	2.4	Select and use appropriate page layout to present information effectively	Pages 86–87
○	3.1	Work accurately and proofread, using software facilities where appropriate for the task	Pages 86–87
○	3.2	Produce information that is fit for purpose and audience using commonly accepted layouts as appropriate	Pages 86–87
○	4.1	Review and modify work as it progresses to ensure the result is fit for purpose and audience	Pages 86–87
○	4.2	Review the effectiveness of the IT tools selected to meet presentation needs	Pages 86–87

edexcel

Assignment tips

- Practise using different formatting techniques for text, numbers and images.
- Make sure you understand when to use the various types of document.
- Always check your work (both spelling and grammar).
- Know when to use different software applications.

DESIGN AND IMAGING SOFTWARE

Have you ever wanted to create a 'Photoshopped' image? Have you ever wondered how people on magazine covers look so perfect? It's no secret that the majority of these images have been edited using a computer and image editing software.

Editing images is much easier than you might think. You don't need to be a computer genius, or even a fantastic artist. You simply need to learn some basic editing techniques to get you on the right path.

In this unit you will:

- Learn to download images from cameras, and from the Internet

- Adjust and edit images, including re-sizing, and cutting out heads

How many magazines do you think 'edit' photos before they are printed?

Choosing your image

The aim of this section is to take a photo of yourself, or a friend, and put the head on someone else's body.

A digital camera is the best method to capture an image of yourself or a friend. It is also very quick to 'download' the image to your computer ('**acquire image**').

A scanner is an effective way of capturing a physical image, such as an image that has already been printed.

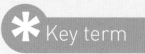

If you don't have a camera or a scanner, instead use the Internet to find a photo of a famous person. (HINT: Try a search engine 'Image Search'.) Right-click the image and 'Save as'. Save this onto your desktop or somewhere you will remember for later.

Alternatively, you could search for an image using a Microsoft Word® clipart library.

Now that you have a photo, we are now ready to begin editing it.

Serif PhotoPlus

We are going to use image editing software to investigate the tools needed to create our very own 'freaky head cut out'.

Serif Photoplus

This is the image we will start with

I have managed to take a rather handsome photo of myself, and we are now ready to start cutting heads.

Activity: Your image

- Before we start, how would you feel about someone 'cutting up' your photo?

- How would you feel if the image used in the example above was your own?

- What could you do to stop your image being used in this book without your permission?

The sort of protection you have is copyright. Your image is 'copywritten', and people must get your permission before they can publish your photo.

Activity: Copyright

Find out about different types of copyright, and how copyright is applied.

Functional skills

Learning about legal terms such as 'copyright' will help develop your skills in English.

Check

- You need to decide whom you are going to photograph, and if they want you to!

- You need to identify what hardware and software you have to get the image you want.

Preparing images

Tools

Can you guess what tools we will be using to cut the head out of a photograph?

The main **tools** we will be using are:

The 'SCALE' tool – this will allow us to scale an image (basically re-size it).

The 'MOVE' tool – this allows us to move the image from one place to another.

The 'MARQUEE' tool or, to be more precise, the 'POLYGON SELECT' tool – this allows us to isolate, and cut out around the head.

Which software?

There are many different types of image editing software in the world. What software you have access to will depend on your school/college.

Whichever software you use to edit images, the names of the tools mentioned above are consistent in all types of image editing software. Basically, they all do the same job, but quite probably in different locations on the screen/software.

Saving your work

Now you have identified what tools we will be using to cut the head out, we must save our work.

As you have probably had some experience with computers, you may have experienced computers unexpectedly crashing, or losing your work. So let's save now.

The software you are using will have the familiar 'File > Save' option. This will allow us to save the image we have 'captured'.

File formats

Have you thought what file format you will save the image as?

File formats are extremely important, especially to graphic designers. The type of file you save will affect the quality of the image. How large the image is in file size (kilobytes and megabytes) will also affect image quality.

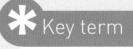

Key term

Tools
The tools within your image editing software. These allow you to manipulate your photo.

Functional skills

Learning technical terms used will help improve your skills in English.

For this task, you will need to save your image as a **JPEG**. You may have also encountered .jpg files which are the same. This is the best format for saving images with lots of colours.

* Key term

JPEG
A file format used for photographic images.

Activity: JPEGs and GIFs

Try to save your image in 'GIF' format. Then try to spot any differences in the quality of the image.

Remember: both of these formats are commonly used.

The JPEG file is at the top, the GIF file is at the bottom. What do you notice about the differences in quality?

✓ Check

- Make a note of the tools you will be using, and identify where they are located in the software you are using.

- Choose the file format you will save the image as, and think of the effect the file format will have.

Editing images

Cropping and moving

You may have noticed that the image you took on your camera is too large, or perhaps the subject is not quite in the right place? Let's 'crop' and 'move' the image.

Crop
A tool to choose an area of an image, and throw away the rest of the image.

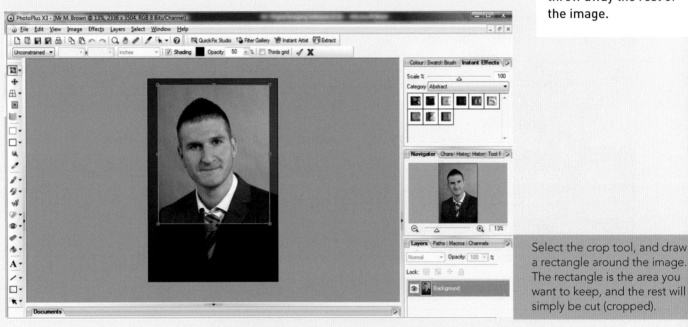

Select the crop tool, and draw a rectangle around the image. The rectangle is the area you want to keep, and the rest will simply be cut (cropped).

Once you have made your selection, hit the 'enter' key to confirm.

You have now cropped your image – well done!

Let's use the 'Polygon Select' tool. This will allow us to 'draw' around the head, and make our selection.

We must select the tool, and then get as close to the image as possible:

Click once, and you will notice that the mouse has a line that is stuck to it … Don't panic, move along the outer edge of the image, and click again. A bit like dot-to-dot.

Keep doing this until you have gone all around the edge of the head.

When you get back to where you started, the path you have created now becomes a 'selection'. (You may need to double click.)

Cutting and pasting

You can now use a familiar tool called 'cut'. This will 'cut' the head from the selection you have made. You can now paste this.

The head has been '**cut and pasted**' from the original photo.

We can now start to place this head over an existing image.

You may need to use the 'scale' tool, to make sure your head is in proportion to the image.

Activity: Effects

Investigate what 'effects' you can use within the software. Try to make the head's skin colour as close to the body's skin colour as you can. It will take some time to experiment with all the different options. (HINT: Look into the Effects options > Image Adjustments.)

Check

- Don't worry if the image you are going to use isn't perfect. You're only going to 'cut it up' anyway.

- Take your time when cutting images.

Magazine covers

Once you are happy with your head cut out and your new body, you can create your very own magazine cover.

Magazine covers need to be attention-grabbing. They should hold the viewer's attention, and finally grab their attention with the words surrounding the image. Just like your favourite magazine front cover.

Shapes

Let's start with **shapes**. Shapes are quite literally shapes of different sizes, angles and design.

I have chosen the star shape, and coloured it red to help make the magazine cover stand out.

Key term

Shapes
Simple shapes that are used to help improve images, such as magazine covers.

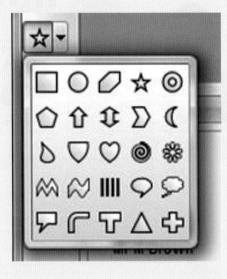

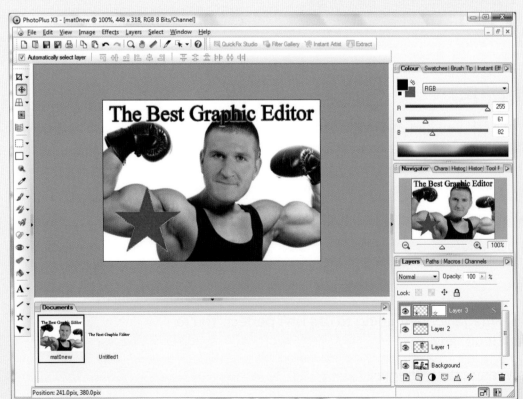

Other tools

Let's use the **text tool** 'T' to type some text over the image.

There are many other tools for you to experiment with.

You should have combined a number of tools to help create your magazine cover, starting with the most basic shapes and text, to exploring how to add 3D text and effects to your image.

As previously mentioned, many different image editing softwares have slightly different ways of completing the same task. They all use the same tools, and the process will be very similar, if not the same.

How did you do?

Before we finish this unit, we need to decide if our final design meets our intended purpose.

We set out to edit an image by cutting out a head, placing that head over someone else's body, and then creating a magazine cover from that. Did you achieve this?

Key term

Text tool
A tool in your image editing software that lets you 'type' text over an image.

Activity: Finalising your cover

What would you change in your magazine cover? Would you be happy seeing your edited image on the front cover of a magazine?

Your final task is to save your magazine cover in JPEG format.

✓ Check

- Adding basic shapes can enhance a magazine cover.

- Text can help the image stand out, and help catch your audience's attention.

ASSESSMENT OVERVIEW

While working through this unit, you will have prepared for completing the following assessment tasks:

○	1.2 Obtain, input and prepare images to meet needs	Pages 92–94
○	1.3 Identify what copyright constraints apply to selected images	Page 93
○	1.4 Use an appropriate file format to save design or image files	Pages 94–95
○	2.1 Identify which manipulation and editing tools and techniques to use	Pages 96–97
○	2.2 Use suitable tools and techniques to create drawings and images	Pages 98–99
○	2.3 Use appropriate tools and techniques to manipulate and edit designs or images	Pages 96–97
○	2.4 Check designs or images meet needs, using IT tools and making corrections as necessary	Page 99

edexcel :::

Assignment tips

- Ask the person's permission, whose image you intend to use for the photo editing.
- Sketch some ideas for your magazine cover. Pen and paper are the best for this.
- Experiment with all the tools available in the software you are using. For example, 'Filters'.
- Don't be afraid to try new techniques. If it doesn't work, you can always 'Undo'.

DESKTOP PUBLISHING SOFTWARE

Desktop publishing (DTP) is a unique and fun way to present information. It combines traditional computing with design and graphics.

It is an exciting area, allowing you flexibility in terms of how you can present information when following requirements or a design brief from a customer. You can express yourself, experiment with different layouts, use various graphics and effects, and really have some fun while doing all of this.

In this unit you will learn to:

- Choose the right designs and page layouts

- Combine text and information in publications

- Edit and format publications

Which of your favourite magazines or newspapers use good DTP design?

Designs and layouts

Desktop publishing (DTP) is a unique area within IT. It lets you combine colours, fonts, logos, pictures and other text features to create different layouts and designs.

Some of the most successful newspapers and magazines use DTP to create their layouts and designs.

Activity: Group discussion

Think of a tabloid newspaper, such as *The Sun*, and think of a broadsheet newspaper, such as *The Independent*.

- Which newspaper would you rather pick up and read?

- Why do you think this is?

Tabloid and broadsheet newspapers

Publication media

There are many different forms of publications that use DTP:

- Published magazines

- Printed and digital newsletters

- Newspapers: both tabloid and broadsheet.

Due to technology, advanced DTP publications can be created digitally, and viewed digitally – for example, online, or directly on your computer. Magazines and newspapers can now be read using digital devices – for example, on laptops, phones or PC tablets.

Types of information

Information comes in many forms. DTP lets you combine different types of information, and make it attractive and appealing for people to read.

The main types of information are:

- Text (like the text you are reading now)

- Images (such as photographs)

- Graphics (symbols and shapes, used to add visual appeal to a layout)

- Video (moving images, such as films)

- Sound (noise and sound, such as music or voice recordings).

✱ Key term

Graphic
Any digital file that is a picture or illustration.

Activity: Think

Think of your favourite magazine, and how it presents information. Does it use simply text, or does it use images and graphics? Think specifically about the front cover.

Check

- DTP lets you create layouts and designs from different information types.

- DTP can be viewed in print and electronic formats.

Page design

The design of a page is very important for DTP. Without design and layout, you might as well be reading a letter. Organising the information into small chunks, emphasised with graphics and images, is key to good DTP.

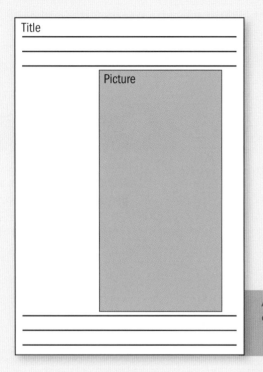

Every document will have a standard size – usually A4. You need to think how you will use the space available, and how you will make your DTP design stand out and look professional.

An example of the layout and design of a DTP page

Case study:
Using DTP in business

Danielle works at a café. She has been asked to design a new menu. She decides to use DTP software to do this as it will look more professional than handwriting the menu.

She decides to include text to describe the different menu items available. She also decides that including some pictures of the food items will make the menu look more interesting. She uses a digital camera to take pictures of the food to include in the menu design.

Activity: Think

Think of a local business you know. Are there any ways you can think of to improve any of their publications using DTP?

Column layout

Most DTP layouts will consist of columns. This is where the page is split into sections.

Most newspapers will use columns. This helps to break up the text and make a large amount of text easier to read.

Columns help to break up the text and make it easier to read.

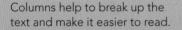
Columns

* Key terms

Orientation
The position of a page – i.e. whether it is portrait or landscape.

Portrait
When the vertical dimension of the page is longer than the horizontal.

Landscape
When the horizontal dimension of the page is longer than the vertical.

! Remember

The orientation of your page is important as well. This can be portrait or landscape.

Activity: Group discussion

Why do you think column layout is a good layout for newspapers?

✓ Check

- Page design is essential to make information look interesting on the page.

- You should think about page size, space and orientation as well as use of columns.

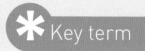
Publishing guidelines

Most organisations will have a **house style**. This is like a theme, where an organisation is associated with particular colours, fonts and logos.

This is also known as branding. Particular colours, fonts and graphics are used to help identify a brand or product. This means that, whenever someone sees the combination in a product or service, they recognise the company it belongs to. Examples include Adidas' three stripes, or Coca-Cola's red can.

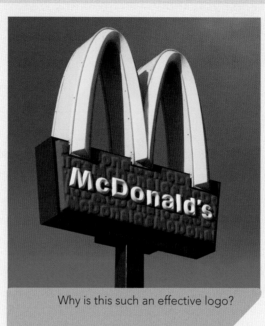

Why is this such an effective logo?

People make these connections through the marketing of a company's house style and brand. Large organisations will have guidelines on how to use this branding. For example, the Adidas name is always spelt out in the same font.

Case study:
Branding

Look at the two companies below – you can see their design brand guidelines.

	Adidas	Coca-Cola
Colour	Black/white	Red/white
Graphics	Three stripes	
Font (similar to)	Avant Garde/Sans serif	Amaze/Serif

Activity: Branding

- What colour do you think of when you hear the word 'McDonalds'?

- What shape/symbol does Nike use?

Templates

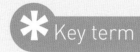

Key term

Template
A document with a pre-set format which can be adapted.

Templates are often used to ensure that branding is consistent, and people do not alter or change any of the properties of the house style.

Templates are helpful in maintaining house styles, but can sometimes be restrictive if you want to alter or edit a design/layout.

You can also use templates available in DTP software. This allows you to create a designed document more easily.

Activity: Think

Using DTP software, look through the templates available. Imagine you were making an invitation for a party. Which template would you use?

Check

- Visual branding is created through DTP.

- House style and templates promote and protect brands.

- Templates can be used in DTP to save time.

Inputting and combining

Inputting information

Generally speaking, 'input' refers to what you put into your computer (put-in – in-put).

Information can be input using various methods:

- Keyboard (typing keys)

- Mouse (clicking or moving something)

- Scanner (scanning a document or photo)

- Microphone (speaking into the computer, where it is recorded).

When information is input into a computer, it can then be further **edited** and proofread.

Combining information

Usually, when you create DTP designs, you are combining information from different sources.

Perhaps you might want to create a magazine-style design. This is likely to have information from an interview from a famous person, and perhaps some graphs and charts from a website on the Internet.

You may also want to include a photo. This may also mean you have to decide how to present and lay out all the information around the photo. This is called 'wrapping'.

You may wish to scan in a photo to use in your work.

Activity: Try

How would you include a photo in the middle of text?

Store and retrieve

After you have created your DTP designs, it is extremely important that you save your work (as it is with any digital file).

Saving your DTP designs sounds obvious, but working in DTP you may have multiple versions of a piece of work. These may have slightly different layouts and designs for the same project.

Giving each of your designs (files) an appropriate file name is vital if you want to find your different designs quickly and easily.

Activity: Think

How would you name different versions (files) of the same DTP project?

Check

- Inputting, combining, storing and retrieving information are all important techniques in DTP.

- You must be aware of copyright law when using other people's information.

DTP techniques

Most software will all use familiar tools. You can apply these to most DTP software:

- Copy/cut and paste: allows you to copy/cut something and paste it somewhere else.

- Undo: allows you to change the size of something: for example, a picture.

- **Layout** guides: such as rulers – these are useful when placing items on your DTP page.

Formatting text

Formatting text is quite simple. Highlight the text you want to change, and then change the font type, size and colour.

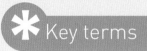

Activity: Try

Can you think of any other things you can change when formatting text?

Styles

Some DTP software use '**styles**', where you can create and pre-define a style for text (for example, Arial, 12pt, Bold). You can then call this style 'Heading 1', and apply this style to any text.

This is a useful technique as it saves time by not having to make all the repetitive choices. Instead, just click 'Heading 1', and everything will format to the style you created.

Activity: Try

In Microsoft Word®, try to create a style. Locate where formatting styles are, and then either create a new style, or edit an existing style.

Manipulating images

Manipulating or editing images is easy and fun. The most basic way to edit an image is to make the image smaller or larger (re-sizing).

You can crop an image, which simply means removing any parts of the image you do not want. This allows you to focus instead on the parts you do want, such as one person in a group photo. (See also Unit 124.)

Control text flow

The flow of text is very important for DTP. Using columns and rows can help break up large pieces of text, and make this information more appealing to the reader.

Text columns can either be a single column (one), or multiple columns (two or more). Text flow can also wrap around images.

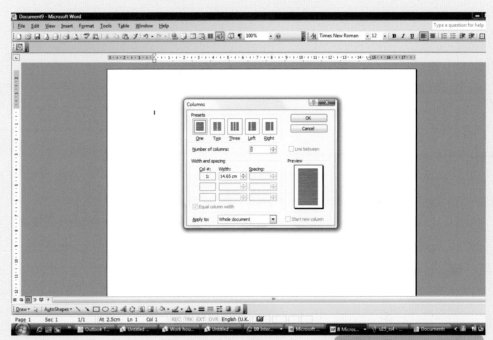

The column menu can be accessed from the format menu.

Activity: Try

Using Microsoft Word®, try to create a three-column, A4, portrait document.

✓ Check

- DTP techniques are the tools you need to create interestingly designed DTP documents.

- You may know some of these already from your work with other software (such as 'cut and paste' in Word).

ASSESSMENT OVERVIEW

While working through this unit, you will have prepared for completing the following assessment tasks:

○	1.1 Identify what types of information are needed	Pages 102–103
○	1.2 Identify what page design and layout will be required	Pages 102–103
○	1.3 Select and use an appropriate page design and layout for publications in line with local guidelines, where available	Pages 104–105
○	1.4 Select and use appropriate media for the publication	Pages 102–103
○	2.1 Input information into publications so that it is ready for editing and formatting	Pages 108–109
○	2.2 Identify copyright constraints on using others' information	Pages 108–109
○	2.3 Organise and combine information of different types or from different sources in line with any copyright constraints	Pages 108–109
○	2.4 Store and retrieve publication files effectively, in line with local guidelines and conventions, where available	Pages 108–109
○	3.1 Identify what editing and formatting to use for the publication	Pages 110–111
○	3.2 Select and use appropriate techniques to edit publications and format text	Pages 110–111
○	3.3 Manipulate images and graphic elements accurately	Pages 110–111
○	3.4 Control text flow within single and multiple columns and pages	Pages 104–105
○	3.5 Check publications meet needs, using IT tools and making corrections as appropriate	Pages 102–103

edexcel :::

Assignment tips

- Think about what information and images you will use for your DTP design.
- Check what images and information you are using, and that you have permission to use them.
- Create draft layouts for your DTP design; even a sketch will help when creating your final layout.
- Save each file with an appropriate file name. This will make finding each of your drafts much quicker.
- Experiment with the tools and techniques available in your DTP software. Some effects are very professional.
- Double-check your DTP design, by using spell check tools, by asking someone else to read it, and of course by re-reading it yourself.

MULTIMEDIA SOFTWARE

Multimedia software is an exciting and very interesting area within IT.

The term 'multimedia' covers a wide area. It is usually associated with graphics, images and 'new age media' such as webpages, magazines and mobile content (apps).

Traditional office applications are not necessarily associated with multimedia software, although they can be adapted and used (for example, using word processing software to create a DTP newsletter).

In this unit you will:

- Plan the content and organisation of multimedia products

- Select and combine multimedia content

- Edit and format multimedia content

- Play and present multimedia

Can you think of when and where multimedia design is used in our everyday lives?

Creating multimedia

Multimedia

Multimedia means just that – many ('multi') different types of media. When you design something for multimedia, you are designing something that can be used across many different media:

- CD-ROMs
- Presentations
- Websites
- Animation
- Video
- Print.

You may need to consider what media your project is aimed at. A brochure could be printed, but it could also be used on a website. The choice of media might have an impact on the content you use.

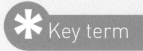
Activity: Group discussion

What possible problems might you face when trying to create a brochure for lots of different media?

Planning a project

Imagine a customer has asked you to create a website for their business, and a brochure. How would you approach and complete such a task?

Planning is essential, and is mostly about preparing how you will undertake such a task, and how you will communicate with the customer. This will help ensure that the customer is given something that they want.

Tools you can use

There are plenty of tools that you can use to help you in the planning and communicating stages with a customer:

- Flow chart: to check what progress and what stage you are at with the project.

- Storyboard: to plan and try out your ideas in a cartoon-like storyboard layout.

- Sketch: to draft your ideas into real drawings. Sketches take an idea and try to make it visual.

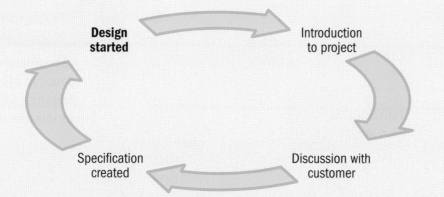

Design started → Introduction to project → Discussion with customer → Specification created →

Planning a project

All of these will help you to communicate with your customer. They will also ensure that everyone involved in the project is happy and aware of the tasks involved and the progress you are making.

Activity: Try

Take a piece of paper, and sketch a draft idea for a layout of a brochure for a small computing company.

✓ Check

- Multimedia is made up of several different types of media.

- Planning and communication are really important when completing a project for a customer.

Functional skills

Learning to plan and communicate with a customer helps to develop your skills in ICT.

Functional skills

Understanding how to approach a project, and how to communicate with customers, will improve your skills in English.

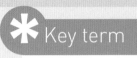
Good project practice

In order to carry out a good project, there are certain practices you should follow. These include following the multimedia **specification**, and being aware of copyright.

The multimedia specification

A multimedia specification is the result of planning and communicating with a customer. It is simply a detailed list of what is required and needed.

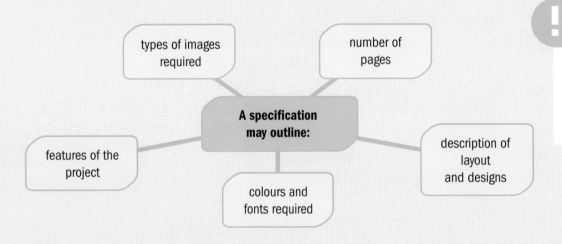

A specification may outline:
- types of images required
- number of pages
- features of the project
- colours and fonts required
- description of layout and designs

Activity: Think

Can you think of anything else that would be helpful to include within the specification?

Copyright

As we have seen in other units, copyright law helps to protect people and the work they create.

When organising your multimedia project, you need to show awareness of copyright, and check you have not broken copyright law.

Copyright law extends to original work created by someone. This can include:

- photos

- text

- drawings

- logos.

If you do use someone's work, you must get their permission and also acknowledge who created it and where you found it.

If you do not do this, and pretend that you created it, this is known as plagiarism, and is very bad practice.

Activity: Think

What types of work should you be aware of copyright for when working on multimedia projects?

Check

- In order to carry out a good project, there are certain practices you should follow.

- A specification will help to keep a project on track.

- You must always follow copyright law to avoid problems with a project.

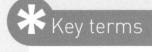
Obtain, input and combine

Inputting information

Inputting information into a computer is quite simple.

Information is **input** into a computer by a user. This user will use an input device such as:

- keyboard

- mouse

- touchscreen

- microphone

- scanner

- web camera.

How you input information into your computer will depend on what facilities/devices your computer has.

Activity: Think

What input device would be best suited when creating a podcast (audio file)?

Combining information

Combining information from different sources, and from different places is the exciting part of using multimedia software. For example, you might be asked to create a poster for a customer. You may be asked to use photos from various resources, perhaps from your own camera, or from a photo stock agency. The customer may also have their own images they would like included in the poster too, as well as some text.

How may you use a webcam to input information?

Activity: Combining information

- Where might you find different images for a poster?

- How could you make sure you avoid breaking any copyright laws?

File format

The **file format** you choose will depend on what you aim to do with your multimedia design.

- For illustrations, a 'vector' format should be used (for example, PDF, SVG, EPS files)

- For photos, a 'bitmap' format should be used (for example, **JPEG**, GIF, PNG files)

- For a graphic for a website, you could use GIF or JPEG files

- For a video for a DVD, you could use AVI or MPEG files

- For a vector animation for a website, you could use SWF files.

Save your files!

Saving files and how and where you save them is an important part of being an efficient and effective multimedia specialist.

A multimedia project may contain a lot of different files, from different locations on the computer. The files you create may also have many different versions, such as different draft layouts and designs.

Functional skills

Learning about different file formats and when you might use them will help develop your skills in **ICT**.

Functional skills

Learning about useful ways of naming and storing files to make finding files quicker and easier will help to develop your skills in **English**.

Activity: Imagine

Find out what your centre's policy on saving files is e.g. where you are supposed to save things, if there's any style you are meant to use for titles. Save a document using these guidelines.

Check

- The way you input information depends on the type of information.

- The file format you use also depends on the type of information.

Multimedia software tools

Edit and publish

Learning about the many different things you can do with multimedia software is very helpful when creating and **publishing** multimedia publications.

Many types of software have similar tools and **techniques**. The most common are:

- the 'move' tool: allows you to move objects around

- the 'scale' tool: allows you to shrink or increase the size of an object

- the 'shapes' tool: allows you to draw different shapes (circular, rectangle).

Other common techniques that can be used in multimedia software are:

- 'undo': allows you to undo your last action, like a rewind button

- 'drag and drop': allows you to click, hold, move and release items (for example, moving a desktop icon)

- 'layout guides': like rulers, but they can be used to help create layouts, such as columns.

Manipulating images

Images and graphics can be **manipulated** and edited. Different multimedia software will have slightly different tools, but the majority of software has the same tools:

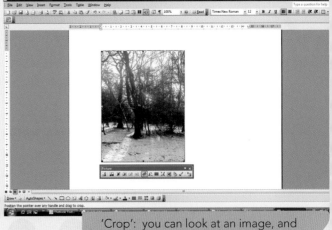

'Crop': you can look at an image, and focus on an area by cutting (cropping) the rest of the image away.

When you resize, or rather 'scale' an image, there is a danger that the image may lose **proportion**. The image can be stretched 'tall', or stretched 'fat'. To avoid this, grab the 'resize handle' from the corner of the image, and then move it. This will help keep the proportions (otherwise known as aspect ratio).

'Scale': you can scale images to be smaller or bigger.

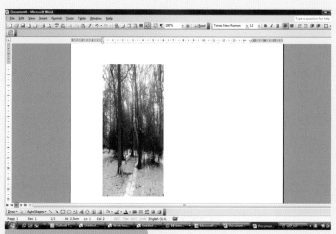

Stretched tall

Stretched fat

Activity: Try

Try to scale and crop an image using whatever software you have available (even word-processing software can be used for this).

Check

- A lot of the techniques available in multimedia editing are found in other software too.

- Manipulating images is an important technique to practise.

At the end of the project...

There are certain things we need to check at the end of a multimedia project to make sure it has gone to plan.

Multimedia outcome

This is the device that your multimedia will show on. In the planning stage of your multimedia project, you should have identified what 'display device' your project is aimed at:

- If your project is a website, will users view it on computers only, or will it be aimed at people viewing it on their mobile devices too? If it is aimed at both, has the layout been considered for mobile devices with small screens?

- If your project is a newsletter, will it be viewed in printed format, or will it be digital so it can be read electronically? If an electronic version, will the digital newsletter contain interactive audio and video features?

Key term

Checklist
A list of items required or needed for the project.

Activity: Other options

Why do we need to think of more than one multimedia outcome (display device), such as printed, digital, small screen, website, etc. when planning our project?

Checking it over

As with all IT work you should make sure you check the work thoroughly. In this case it should match the project specification set out at the start of the project (which was agreed by both you and the customer). The customer should be happy with the final project.

Finally, you should visually check the whole project and spot any mistakes you may have made.

Mistakes are common, so don't panic when you find one. Look for:

- Typing mistakes, called 'typos'

- Missing full stops or commas

- Grammar and sentence structure

- Images, and that they are in the correct position.

Case study:
Project checklist

Christine works for a multimedia design company. The company specialises in animation design for websites. Christine is very involved in the management and running of projects and makes it a special priority to check everything extremely carefully at the end of the process to ensure that all has gone to plan.

She has a checklist that she makes from the project specification to make sure she has checked everything required for each project.

Activity: Quality check

If you did Christine's job, what other ways would you make sure that all work was completed perfectly?

Check

- It's really important to finish a project as well as you have started it off.

- Checking work against a project specification and for more basic spelling and grammar mistakes is vital.

Functional skills

Learning to 'proofread' (check) your work for spelling and grammatial errors will help you develop your skills in English.

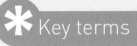
Play and present multimedia

Multimedia outcomes

Playing and presenting multimedia projects is what multimedia is all about. Some customers may already know, and request that you design a multimedia project for a specific display device.

📁 Case study:
Web design

Thérèse works for a web design company. This means the display device for her media is the Internet and computer screens. Whenever she works on a website design project she needs to consider a number of different things, such as:

- Download speeds

- Size of users' screens

- Size of the images to display

- How much of the screen to use.

◎ Activity: Designing a game

Imagine you are a multimedia designer working for a games design company. Can you think of any restrictions of the display device when designing a multimedia game for a mobile phone?

Have you played any games on a mobile phone?

Display device features

When you know what display device(s) your multimedia project is aimed for, you can begin to integrate this into your design.

Display device features might include:

- Touchscreen: user can physically touch the screen

- Small or large screen: users can see more or less of the screen

- Audio: user can listen to sound

- Colour: user can see different colours

- Play, pause, rewind: user can interact with the multimedia

- High definition: user can see greater detail of the multimedia.

You also need to think about how users will navigate your design.

Activity: Effective features

How would you use some of the above features when creating a website for an estate agent?

You can include items such as navigation and menus. This can add a level of interactivity for the user.

The display device that your users will use can affect your multimedia project, and you need to consider if the display device can be used to improve your multimedia project.

! Remember

Users may want to change the display settings of a multimedia project:

- Some users may have sensitive eyes, and want to turn down the brightness

- Some users may prefer to see using a high contrast

- Some users may be hard of hearing, and need to turn up the volume.

There are many reasons users may want to change and customise display settings. It may be a personal preference, or perhaps to do with a person's special needs.

✓ Check

- Different display devices can affect your multimedia project.

- You need to think about navigation and other interactive features for users.

ASSESSMENT OVERVIEW

While working through this unit, you will have prepared for completing the following tasks:

○	1.1	Use simple techniques to plan and communicate the content and organisation of multimedia products	Pages 114–115
○	1.2	Identify the type of multimedia outcome to meet requirements	Pages 114–115
○	1.3	Identify what is required in the specification	Pages 114–115
○	1.4	Identify copyright or other constraints for using others' information	Pages 116–117
○	2.1	Use an appropriate input device to enter content for multimedia outcomes	Pages 118–119
○	2.2	Combine information of different types or from different sources for multimedia outcomes	Pages 118–119
○	2.3	Identify the file format and storage media to use	Pages 118–119
○	2.5	Store and retrieve multimedia files effectively, in line with local guidelines and conventions where available	Pages 118–119
○	3.1	Select and use appropriate techniques to edit and format multimedia outcomes	Pages 120–121
○	3.2	Manipulate images and graphic elements accurately	Pages 120–121
○	3.3	Check multimedia outcomes meet needs, using IT tools and making corrections as necessary	Pages 122–123
○	4.1	Identify what display device to use for multimedia outcomes	Pages 122–123
○	4.2	Use appropriate techniques to navigate and display multimedia outcomes	Pages 124–125
○	4.3	Control the playback of multimedia files	Pages 124–125
○	4.4	Adjust display settings to meet needs	Pages 124–125

edexcel

Assignment tips

- Planning is key to producing an outstanding multimedia project.
- Beware of using images and text from the Internet. Check who material belongs to and that you have permission to use it.
- Naming your files will help when trying to locate various designs. It will make things quicker and more efficient when you are looking for the right file.
- Think about where and how your multimedia project will be displayed. It will help improve your project.

PRESENTATION SOFTWARE

Presentations can be used for a number of different purposes, such as communicating information, education and promotion.

The ability to create good presentations can be useful in a number of situations throughout your life. You may need to use them for job interviews, in the workplace and perhaps even recreationally (for example, to produce a presentation out of holiday photos).

In this unit you will:

- Input and combine text and other information in slides

- Structure, edit and format slides

- Prepare slides for presentation

How effective do you think this slide is?

PRESENTATION SOFTWARE

Creating presentation slides

As with most documents that can be created on a computer, presentation **slides** can contain a mixture of different types of information. The slides can display text, numbers, images and graphics effectively.

Text boxes

In order to enter text onto a slide you need to insert a **text box**. A text box can be created by selecting 'Insert' and then 'Text Box'. Then click on the slide where you would like to begin typing. This will insert a text box on the slide so that you can now type text onto the slide.

Adding images, music and video

Inserting a picture into a slide

Images can also be added to a slide. Select 'Insert', and you can choose from 'Picture', 'Chart' or 'Table'.

Music and video clips can also be added to presentations; these can also be added from the 'Insert' menu.

Different types of information can be combined on presentation slides, such as having graphics alongside the text.

Adding a new slide

You can have as many slides as you wish in your presentation. In order to add a new slide, select 'New Slide' from the 'Home' menu, as shown:

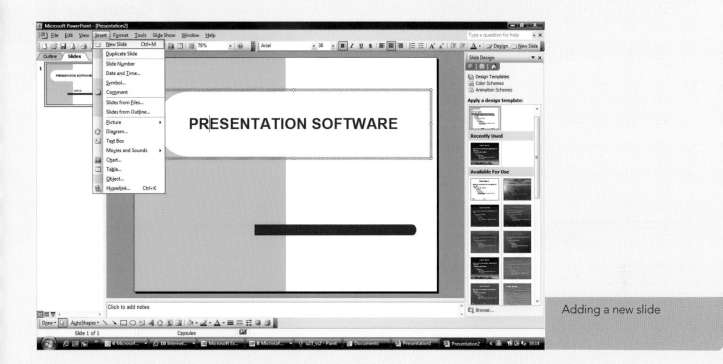

Adding a new slide

Activity: Create a presentation

Create your own presentation on your favourite hobby using a mixture of text and images.

! Remember

Always follow copyright guidelines when using someone else's information.

✓ Check

- Slides can contain many different types of information.

- You can have as many slides as you like in a presentation.

Storing and retrieving files

Saving files

It is extremely important to save your files properly so you can find them again.

Presentation **software** lets you name and save files in the same way as other computer software packages.

Click on the 'Save' button, which is found on the toolbar at the top of the screen.

Try to give each file you create a different filename so you will recognise what the document is without having to open each one to find out. For example, the presentation shown above could be called 'music presentation'.

Once you have saved your document you can then exit the presentation software package without losing the document, as it can be reopened at any time.

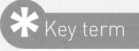

Key term

Software
The applications you use on your computer.

Save button

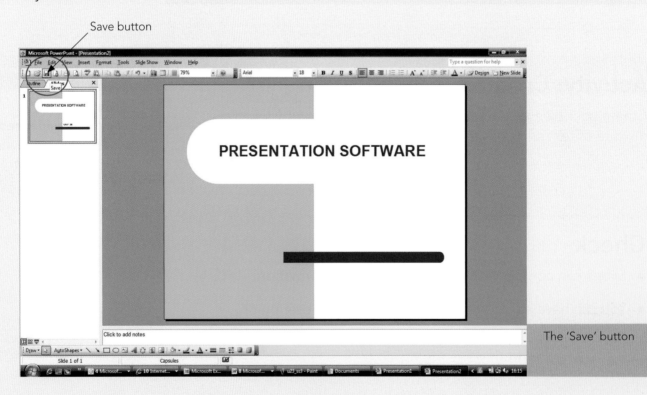

The 'Save' button

Reopening files

To reopen a document, start the presentation software package and select the 'Open' button, which is also located on the toolbar at the top of the screen. You can then locate the file you saved previously.

Activity: Adding music to a presentation

Try to add some music to your presentation and experiment with different colours.

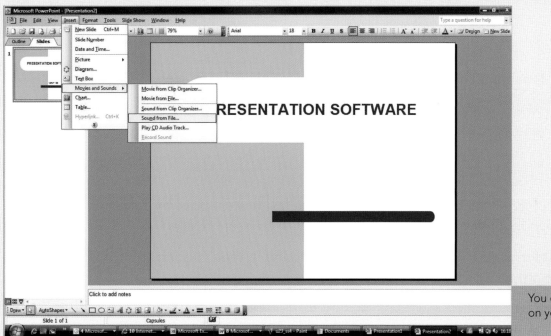

You can add sounds from a file on your computer or a CD.

Check

- You can save and retrieve your presentation files in the same way as you do with other software, such as Microsoft Word®.

- It is important to give files a name that suits their content.

Editing your slides

Information can be edited in a number of ways by selecting the piece of information that you wish to change and then selecting the required **formatting** tool.

Moving text or images

The easiest method to move pieces of text and images around on slides is to use the 'drag and drop' option:

- Hover near the edge of the image or text box you wish to move, and wait until the cursor changes.

- While holding down the left mouse button, drag the item to its new position.

You can move text or images by using **cut and paste**.

- Select the information you wish to move, then click on the 'Cut' button.

- Click the area where you wish the information to be moved to, then click on the 'Paste' button.

Mistakes

If you edit a document by accident, you can undo the last few changes by clicking on the 'Undo' button.

You can delete information from a document by selecting it, then clicking on the 'Delete' button.

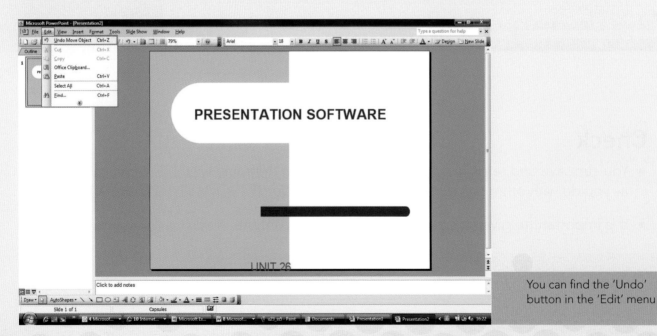

You can find the 'Undo' button in the 'Edit' menu

Text boxes

You can also change the shape and size of the text boxes relatively easily.

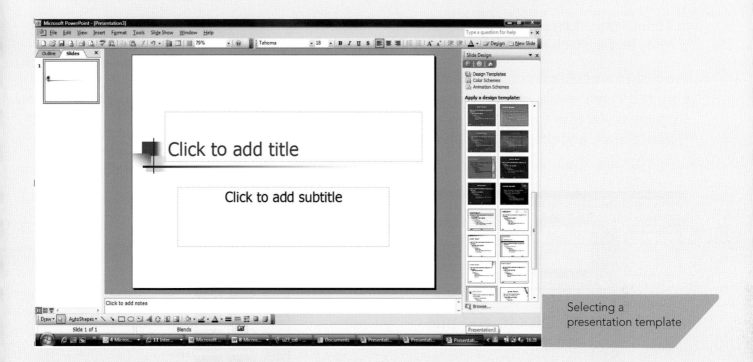

Selecting a presentation template

Activity: Presentation template

Open a presentation **template** and start to edit some of its features. For example:

- Rearrange some of the features

- Resize any images.

✱ Key term

Template
A document with a preset format which can be adapted.

✓ Check

- You can move and resize material in your slides.

- You can correct mistakes as you go along.

Shapes and colours

In addition to adding text and images to your slides, you can add lines, **shapes** and even change the colour of different areas of the slides.

In order to add lines and other basic shapes to your slides, select 'Shapes' from the 'Insert' menu as shown in the screenshot below. Then select the shape that you wish to add, click on the slide where you would like the shape to start, and drag the shape to the correct size.

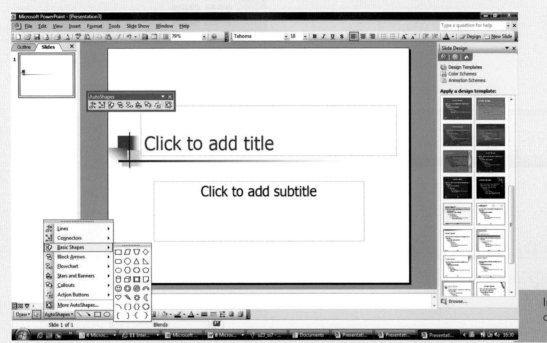

Inserting lines and other basic shapes

◎ Activity: Add shapes

Create a presentation and try adding a shape to each slide.

Adding colour

Colour can be added to all areas of the slide. To change the background colour of a slide go to the 'Format' tab on the toolbar at the top of the screen and select 'Background', then select a colour as shown below.

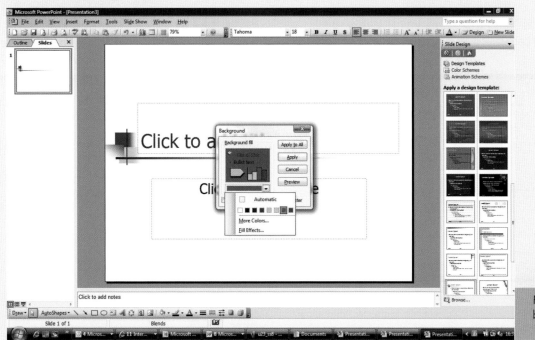

Formatting the background of a slide

The 'Apply to All' button lets you apply your chosen colour to all the slides in your presentation.

Activity: Change the background

Try changing the background colour on all the slides in your presentation.

Remember

You can also use the templates in the presentation software to save time.

Check

- You can make your slides more interesting with lines, shapes and colours.

Preparing slides for presentation

Once you have created all the slides you need to make a presentation, you need to consider a few things so that the presentation works.

The order that the slides appear in the presentation can be changed by selecting 'Slide Sorter' from the 'View' menu.

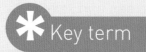

Key term

Slideshow
The way in which the slides will appear during a presentation.

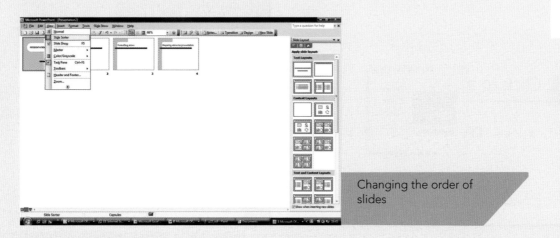

Changing the order of slides

You can view the presentation as a **slideshow** by selecting 'Slideshow' from the 'View' menu. You can move to the next slide by clicking anywhere on the screen, or by pressing 'Enter'.

Rehearse timings

As part of your preparation you may wish to 'Rehearse Timings' (found in the 'Slideshow' menu). This allows you to display the slides on screen as they would appear during the presentation, while you practise your speech. With this tool, you can set the delay in moving onto the next slide. This means you can set the right amount of time for you to talk about each slide.

Rehearse timings as part of your preparation.

Handouts

Once the presentation has been finished, it is useful to print out the slides as **handouts** which can be given to the audience.

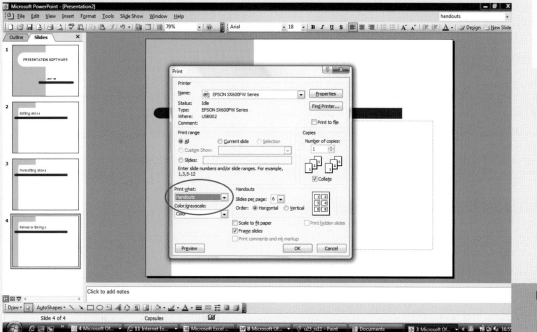

How to make handouts

Activity: Printing handouts

Open up a presentation you have started and print out the slides in the handout format.

Check

- It is important to practise presentations before you give them.

- Your audience might like handouts of the slides to follow during the presentation, or to use afterwards.

ASSESSMENT OVERVIEW

While working through this unit, you will have prepared for completing the following assessment tasks:

○	1.1	Identify what types of information are required for the presentation	Pages 128–129
○	1.2	Select and use different slide layouts as appropriate for different types of information	Pages 128–129
○	1.3	Enter information into presentation slides so that it is ready for editing and formatting	Pages 128–129
○	1.4	Identify copyright or other constraints on using others' information	Pages 128–129
○	1.5	Combine information of different forms or from different sources for presentations	Pages 128–129
○	1.6	Store and retrieve presentation files effectively, in line with local guidelines and conventions where available	Pages 130–131
○	2.1	Identify what slide template to use	Pages 132–133
○	2.2	Select and use an appropriate template to structure slides	Pages 132–133
○	2.3	Select and use appropriate tools and techniques to edit slides	Pages 132–133
○	2.4	Select and use appropriate tools and techniques to format slides	Pages 132–133
○	3.1	Identify how to present slides to meet needs and communicate effectively	Pages 134–135
○	3.2	Prepare slides for presentation	Pages 136–137
○	3.3	Check presentation meets needs, using IT tools and making corrections as appropriate	Pages 136–137

edexcel

Assignment tips

- Try to practise as many of the techniques in this unit as possible using presentation software.
- If you are working on a presentation, add more information using as many of the tools mentioned in this unit as you can. You could add photos, for example.
- If you need to give a presentation, try rehearsing it in front of a friend.
- Always check your slides thoroughly to make sure you look professional.

SPREADSHEET SOFTWARE

No matter which industry you choose to work in, you will come across spreadsheets in one form or another. You can use a spreadsheet to manipulate (change to meet user needs) data and even present information.

Spreadsheets can be used to store and display data in many different formats, including a table or a graphical format such as a chart or a graph. You can use spreadsheet software to store financial data (such as staff wages), data records (such as your study grades) and graphs (to indicate how much you spend on different things throughout the week).

In this unit, you will learn to:

- Enter and edit different information in a spreadsheet

- Use formulas within a spreadsheet

- Use tools and techniques to improve a spreadsheet

A graphical representation of cash flow. What other uses do spreadsheets have?

Cells, rows and columns

A spreadsheet file is made up of lots of individual **cells**. Each cell is stored in **rows** and **columns**. This makes the file look like a very big grid. You can enter both numbers and text into the cells. This allows you to store a lot of different data in one place.

The screenshots below investigate what each of the following look like:

● Cells

● Rows

● Columns.

Cell

As you can see from the screenshot below, there are many cells on this page. We have chosen just one. The highlighted yellow area is one single cell.

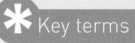

＊ Key terms

Cell (spreadsheet)
An individual square within a spreadsheet.

Row (spreadsheet)
Cells that are positioned next to each other in a horizontal line.

Column (spreadsheet)
Cells that are positioned next to each other in a vertical line.

An example of a cell

◎ Activity: Cells

How many **cells** can you see in the screenshot above?

Row

As you can see from the screenshot opposite, there are many rows on this page. We have just chosen one – row 2. (The row number is given on the left-hand side of the diagram.) The highlighted yellow area is one single row.

An example of a row

Activity: Rows

How many rows can you see in the screenshot opposite?

Column

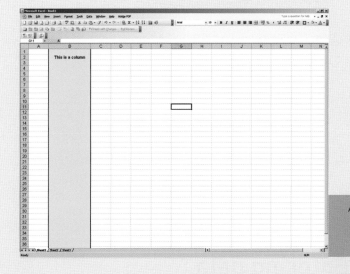

As you can see from this screenshot below, there are many columns on this page. We have chosen just one – column B. (The column letter is given at the top of the diagram.) The highlighted yellow area is one single column. Did you notice that the columns are vertical?

An example of a column

Activity: Columns

How many columns can you see in the spreadsheet opposite?

 Functional skills

Counting the cells, rows and columns could help you develop your skills in **Mathematics**.

✓ Check

- Spreadsheets are made up of many cells.
- Cells are stored in rows and columns.

Enter and edit...

A spreadsheet allows the user to store different information and data in different cells, rows and columns. Spreadsheet software also allows us to **enter**, **edit**, clear and copy data into and from different cells. Below we will look at how to carry out these tasks.

Enter

To enter data, first click on the cell you would like to enter your data. Make sure there is a black box on the outside of the cell you want to store your data in (as shown in the screenshot below). Once the cell is highlighted, click on the area shown in the red circle. You can now use the keyboard to enter your data. Once all your data is in the cell, press 'enter' on the keyboard to ensure the data is entered into the cell.

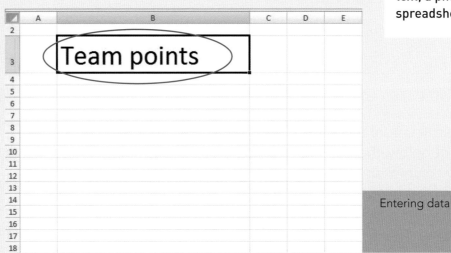

Entering data

Activity: Entering data

Create a new spreadsheet and enter your name in the cell B3.

Edit

It is possible to change any data that you have entered into a cell. Click on the cell that contains the data you want to change. Then click on the writing shown in the red circle in the screenshot opposite. You can click anywhere within the text and re-type different data in the same cell. This is known as editing information.

Activity: Editing data (1)

Using the spreadsheet file that you created for the activity above, try to add your middle name to cell B3.

Editing data

Activity: Editing data (2)

- Using the spreadsheet you created for the activity above, enter the names of five people in your class. You should write only their first initial and their surname (for example, K Sharpe).

- Then edit the list to include their first names as well as their surnames (for example, Kenny Sharpe).

Check

- When you insert new information into a spreadsheet, you are entering information.

- When you change existing information in a spreadsheet, you are editing information.

Clear, copy and find

In the previous topic you learnt how to enter and edit data into a cell. You may also need to remove data from a cell. This is known as clearing information (or deleting). You can do this in a similar way to editing information. First, you need to click on the cell with the data stored within it. Then you can delete information with the 'Delete' key.

Key terms

Data
Information, often combines both numbers and letters.

Clearing
Deleting information (for example, from the cell of a spreadsheet).

Activity: Deleting data

Open the spreadsheet you created in the activity on page 142. Try to delete your name from cell B3.

Copy

You can also replicate (copy) data. This allows you to type the information in once only, instead of having to repeatedly type it. As always when you need to change data in spreadsheets, you need to click on the appropriate cell. Once the black outline appears around the cell, you can copy the data.

- Click on the 'Edit' menu and select the 'Copy' option.

- Click on the cell you want to copy the data into, click the 'Edit' option again and then choose 'Paste'.

- You will see that the same information now also appears in a different cell.

Activity: Try

- Write your name in cell B2.

- Edit cell B2 by putting a title at the start of your name.

- Copy your name from cell B2 and paste it into cell D2.

- Delete your name from cell B2.

Find

Imagine that you had to find one piece of information out of a hundred in a spreadsheet. This could take a long time to find, especially if the information is very similar. To make life easier, you can search for individual data by clicking 'Edit' then 'Find'. This will make the search box shown in the screenshot below appear.

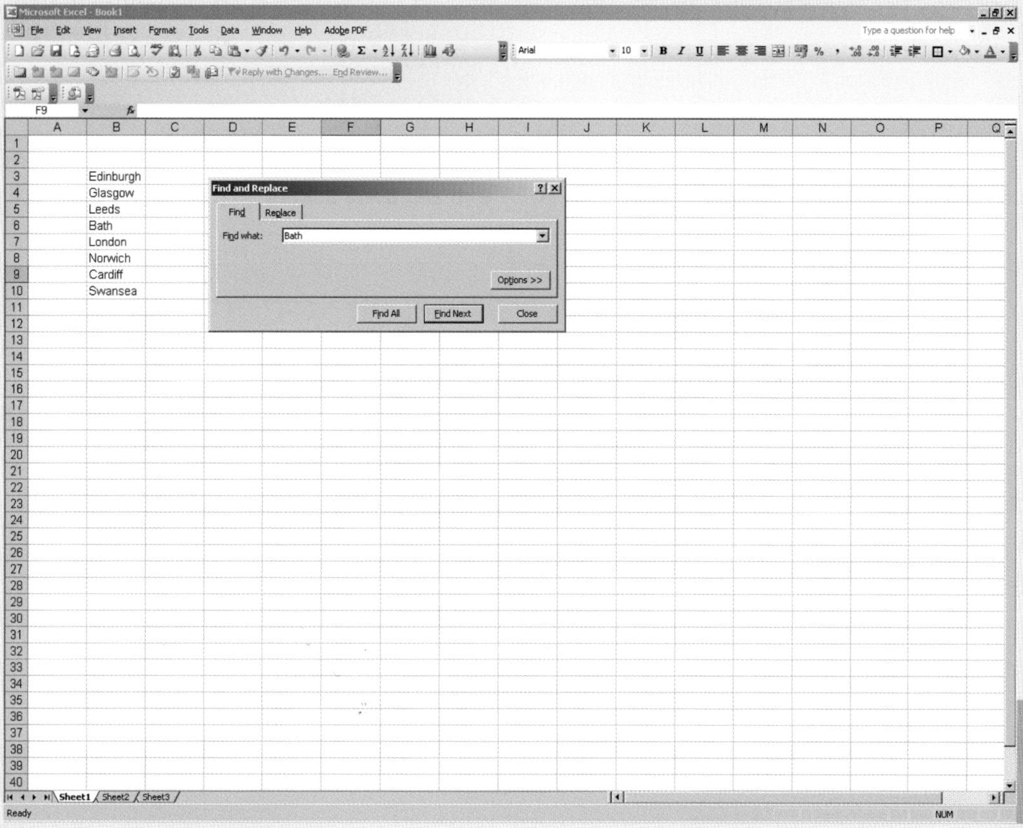

Finding data

Activity: Find next

Using the search box as shown above, type the information you want to find, then click the 'Find Next' button. What happens next?

✓ Check

- You can copy and delete information within spreadsheets.

- You can find information easily in a spreadsheet using the 'Find' box.

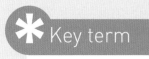

Graphs and charts

Spreadsheets do not just store data in different cells. Spreadsheet software also lets you create different graphs and charts. This will allow more complex information to be shown as **graphics**. Spreadsheets can also carry out mathematical calculations for us too. This means that the user can let the computer do the hard work.

> **✳ Key term**
>
> **Graphic**
> Any digital file that is a picture or illustration.

Bar charts

Bar charts can be used to show many different types of information. The most popular use for bar charts is to show different amounts of information during different times. The example opposite shows the number of muffins sold in a small bakery business in the different months of the year.

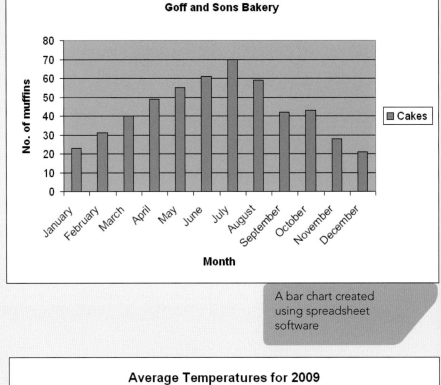

A bar chart created using spreadsheet software

Line graphs

Line graphs can be used to show information that has a continued pattern. In other words, the information shown is connected. The example opposite shows the average temperature across the calendar year. The continuous line links all the months together.

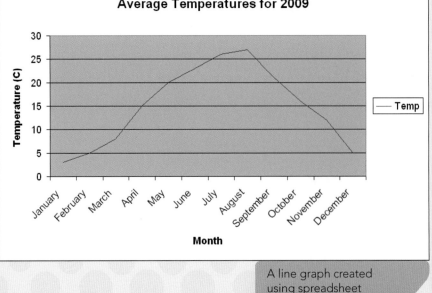

A line graph created using spreadsheet software

Pie charts

Pie charts can be used to show information in fractions. The example shown below indicates a class's favourite flavour of milkshake. You can see that different flavours have their own section.

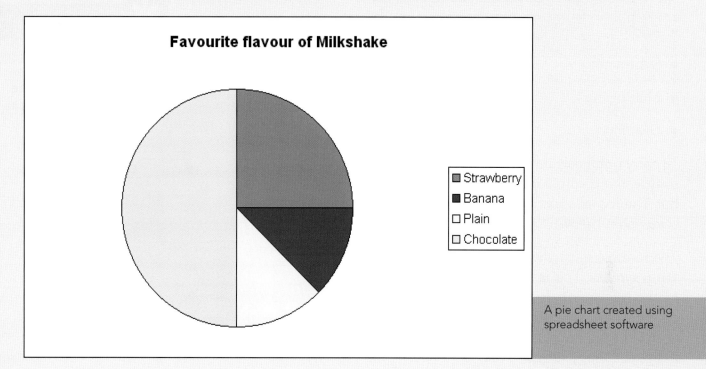

Favourite flavour of Milkshake

☐ Strawberry
■ Banana
☐ Plain
☐ Chocolate

A pie chart created using spreadsheet software

Activity: Think

Can you think of the different types of information you can show in a bar chart, a line graph and a pie chart?

Check

- Information can be displayed in lots of different ways, depending on what type it is.

Formulas

Spreadsheets can make calculations, such as:

- Adding

- Subtracting

- Multiplying

- Dividing.

To carry out a calculation you need to type the **formula** into the formula bar. The formula bar is shown in the screenshot below.

The formula must always begin with the = symbol. This is then followed by the calculation: for example, =5+5. When you press 'Enter', the answer of the formula will appear in the cell that you typed the formula in.

The blue circle in the screenshot above shows the formula that has been entered into cell B2. The red circle shows the answer of the formula entered into cell B2.

Notice that only the result of the formula is shown in the cell. The formula itself is hidden unless you click on the cell that contains the formula.

Key term

Formula
A sequence of commands that make a sum (for example, in spreadsheets).

An example of a formula

Formula results

Case study:
Recording information

Functional skills

Creating a formula in a spreadsheet will help you to improve your skills in Mathematics.

Claire has a market stall selling flowers. She records the number of each flower sold each day and records this information for each day that the stall is open. Claire stores her information in a spreadsheet shown below.

	A	B	C	D	E	F	G	H	I	J
			Monday	Tuesday	Wednesday	Thursday	Friday	Saturday	WEEKLY TOTAL	
5		Geberas	2	3	2	4	7			
6		Daisies	12	13	10	13	14	8		
7		Roses	15	10	14	12	6	11		
8		Tulips	20	23	13	15	10	16		
9		Lillies	5	10	12	14	15	12		
10		DAILY TOTAL								

Claire's flower stall information

Activity: Help Claire!

Claire would like the shaded areas of the spreadsheet completed. This way she can quickly see the weekly total sales of each flower and how many flowers she sells each day. Enter the formula to help Claire complete the spreadsheet.

✔ Check

- You can make calculations quickly and easily in spreadsheets using formulas.

Presenting information

As you have seen from previous topics, spreadsheets allow you to enter data, edit data, perform calculations and even produce different charts and graphs. The look of spreadsheets can be improved by adding colours and borders to different cells. In addition, you can change the size of the page to better suit the information it contains.

Formatting cells

You can **format** the appearance of individual cells by adding borders. You can even change the background colour.

You can also align the text in different areas of the cell. **Alignment** means the position of the text – text can be set to align to the left, to the right or to the centre.

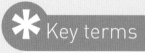

Key terms

Formatting
The way information is presented.

Alignment
The position of material on a page.

D4		f_x			
A	**B**			**C**	**D**
1					
2					
3	Left align				
4		Centre align			
5			Right align		
6					
7					
8					
9					
10					
11					
12					

Examples of text alignment

All financial information should be aligned to the right. If needed, you can change the colour of the text – for example, you could highlight important information in red.

Formatting rows and columns

Sometimes the information that you enter into a cell can be too long for the size of the cell. This could cause problems because you can't easily view all of the information. Fortunately, you can change the size of rows and columns to meet the needs of the data. You can apply a border to a complete row or column, just as you can to individual cells.

Formatting charts and graphs

You have already seen that you can change the appearance of individual cells, complete rows and complete columns. You can also change the appearance of the charts and graphs by formatting their titles, colours and sizes.

It is also possible to change the type of graph. Can you remember the different types of graphs and charts we explored earlier in this chapter?

! Remember

You can also change:

- the size of the page
- the size of the margins
- the orientation of the page.

Activity: Try

Using a new spreadsheet file, try changing the colour of different cells, then adding a border to the different colours you created.

Check

- The appearance of a cell, row, column and a page can be changed.
- You can align text in three different ways within each cell.

ASSESSMENT OVERVIEW

While working through this unit, you will have prepared for completing the following assessment tasks:

○	1.1	Identify what numerical and other data is needed and how the spreadsheet should be structured to meet needs	Pages 140–141
○	1.2	Enter and edit numerical and other data accurately	Pages 142–143
○	1.3	Store and retrieve spreadsheet files effectively, in line with local guidelines and conventions where available	Pages 142–143
○	2.1	Identify how to summarise and display the required information	Pages 144–145
○	2.2	Use functions and formulas to meet calculation requirements	Pages 148–149
○	2.3	Use spreadsheet tools and techniques to summarise and display information	Pages 150–151
○	3.1	Select and use appropriate tools and techniques to format spreadsheet cells, rows and columns	Pages 142–143
○	3.2	Identify which chart or graph type to use to display information	Pages 146–147
○	3.3	Select and use appropriate tools and techniques to generate, develop and format charts and graphs	Pages 146–147
○	3.4	Select and use appropriate page layout to present and print spreadsheet information	Pages 150–151
○	3.5	Check spreadsheet information meets needs, using IT tools and making corrections as appropriate	Pages 150–151

edexcel

Assignment tips

- Practise entering, editing and deleting information from different cells.
- Understand when to use different charts and graphs to represent different types of information. It will be very helpful if you practise creating graphs and charts.
- Experiment with different colours and borders for individual cells, rows and columns.
- Practise building formulas to carry out calculations.

WEBSITE SOFTWARE

As the Internet grows and new technologies are developed, websites are becoming more and more popular. There are currently millions of websites available to view.

Websites can be used for many different subjects and areas. Different areas can include businesses, sports teams, social networking and even individual websites. Websites can be as simple as one page or very complex, with hundreds of pages.

In this unit, you will learn to:

- Design and build webpages

- Format different webpages

- Publish webpages on the Internet

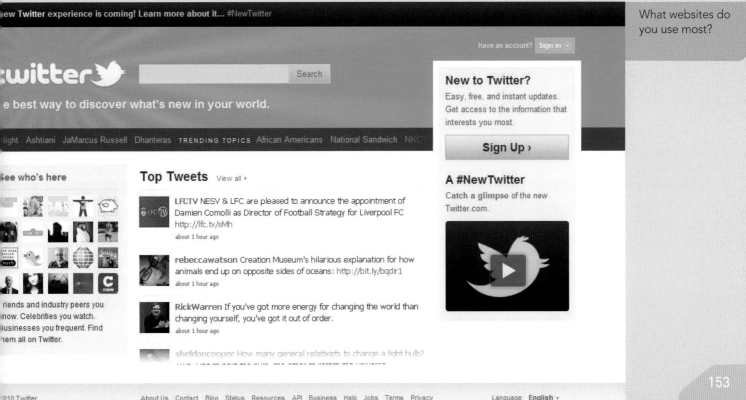

What websites do you use most?

Purpose and target audience

Websites are built for many different reasons and for many different people. Each website has its own look and feel. Before creating a website, you need to take the following into account:

- The **purpose** of the website
- The **target audience** of the website.

Purpose of a website

Every website that is currently on the Internet has been built for a particular reason. Reasons for building a website will vary hugely. A website might:

- advertise a business
- sell a company's products
- help an individual person to keep in contact with friends and family.

The examples above will result in completely different websites being built. It is important that the correct website is built for the correct purpose.

Target audience

When building a website you need to think about who is going to use the website. Different types of users will have different requirements.

There are a number of ways you can find out what the audience wants within the website:

- You can ask potential users to complete a questionnaire.
- You can interview the potential audience to gain a better understanding of their requirements.

✱ Key terms

Purpose
The reason behind doing something (for example, creating a website).

Target audience
The people who are most likely to use a website.

! Remember

You need to find out the aims and key features of each website you build.

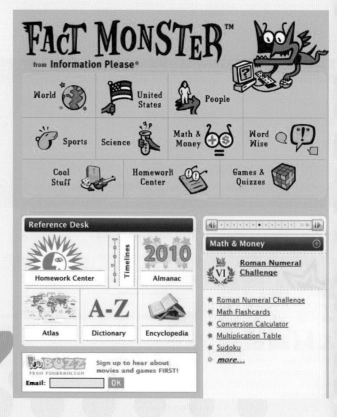

Children want websites to be bright and colourful.

Case study:

Website questionnaires

Talia and David have been asked to look into what might be needed for a website for their school's art department. The website will show the learners' work and let all learners know of any breaking news from the department. Talia and David decided they needed to know much more about their audience before outlining what they thought the website might need.

They came up with a questionnaire for the whole school to complete. This asked a number of questions about what people expected from the website, including how it should look, the kind of information it should have, etc.

Activity: Identifying a target audience

Imagine you have a similar task to Talia and David. Can you think of three questions you could put on the questionnaire?

Check

- It is important to understand the purpose of a website.
- Each website will have a target audience.

Website templates

As the demand for websites keeps on growing, the amount of experts also grows. Some experts create webpages and allow other developers to use their work free of charge. These files are known as **website templates**.

Website templates can be used as a foundation to create webpages. You will be able to find website templates on the Internet. They come in many different styles and colours.

Key terms

Website template
The outline of a webpage that has been created previously.

Select
To find and choose an item.

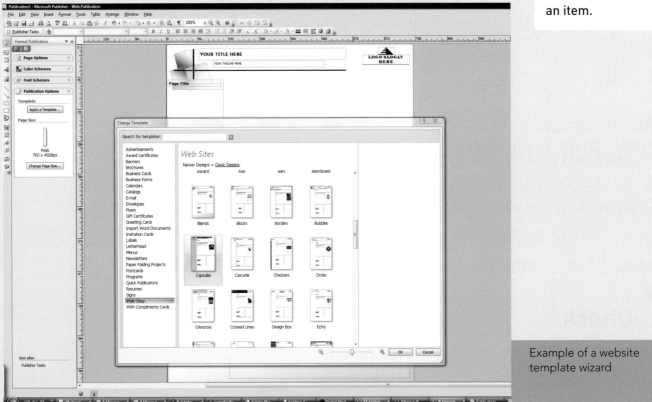

Example of a website template wizard

Elements of a template

These elements are combined to make a webpage:

Body text: the main font used for the majority of text on a webpage
Images: photographs or other images
Captions: text attached to images
Tables: format for organising the information on the webpage.

Professional software companies also create website templates for their users to edit and use. The screenshot below shows an example of a professional software company's template. As you can see in the screenshot opposite, there are many different options available to the user. The user simply selects which website template they wish to use and clicks 'Create' or 'OK'. The webpage is then created.

A demonstration of a webpage created from a template

Activity: Find a webpage template

Using the Internet, research and save a webpage template. Remember to be careful which files you save and use.

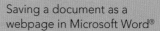

Saving a document as a webpage in Microsoft Word®

Webpages come in a variety of file types. You could use Microsoft Publisher® to create a template if you have access to it. Alternatively, you could create a design for a webpage in Microsoft Word® and save it as a webpage.

Check

- You can create a webpage very quickly using a pre-created template.

- There are many different styles of templates.

Organising and planning your website

When creating websites you can use many different pieces of information within each page. However, a vast amount of information can become very confusing. If the website is built without any forethought, this confusion can carry over to the user of the website.

To avoid such confusion, you should **organise** and **plan** the layout of your website. You can also plan the order in which you are going to develop the website.

Planning

Planning could include a list of events you wish to carry out. The more detailed the list, the easier it will be to follow the list.

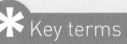

Activity:
Navigating a website

Visit a website (the BBC News website is a good example). Explore the website, taking note of the different types of **navigation** (e.g. image links, hyperlinks, search boxes).

Organise

Organising can include placing all the images needed for the website in an appropriate folder. This will help you to organise which page is going to be linked to another. Producing a diagram of each page can help achieve this.

---

* Key terms

Organise
To put things in a sensible order to make things easier for yourself.

Plan
To work out what you need to do before you do it.

Navigation
The routes you can use to explore a website.

Case study:
Linking webpages

A local shop has an idea for a website. They want to have five pages within their website. The pages are as follows:

- Home page
- Staff members
- Fresh produce
- Bakery
- Books/magazines.

Each page is to link to the home page. The staff members page can link only to the home page. The books/magazines page links only to the home page and staff members page. The bakery and fresh produce pages link to all pages except for the staff members page.

Activity: Produce a diagram

Produce a diagram for the local shop to show how each page links to another. Remember to stick within the guidelines stated within the case study.

Check

- It is important to plan and organise your website.
- You must remember not to copy other people's work without their permission.

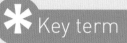

Types of file

As with all software, there are certain requirements and restrictions in terms of which **file type** can be used when saving webpages. You also need to consider which file type you use when including text files, images, sound and graphics within webpages.

Text files

Text files are used to store text-based information. For example, an instruction manual could be stored as a text file. Types of text files include:

- Rich Text File (RTF): a text file that can be stored in most versions of word processing software and used in almost all types of operating system. RTFs can be easily edited.

- .[dot] or .doc file: a Microsoft Word® file that can be used within most operating systems.

- Portable Document File (PDF): PDFs are relatively small in size and can reduce the amount of storage space needed. This makes them ideal for a website. Unfortunately, it is very difficult to edit PDFs.

Image files

The majority of websites contain images within them. These help to improve the appearance of a website. Types of image file include:

- Joint Photographic Experts Group (JPEG): a special file format used for storing images, JPEG files are often recommended for use within a website due to their small size. A lot of digital cameras use the JPEG file format.

- Tagged Image File Format (TIFF): TIFF files can be used to store images across multiple operating systems. Typically TIFF files store images in millions of tiny pixels.

- PhotoShop Document (PSD): a file format used to store images created in Adobe® PhotoShop® software.

✳ Key term

File type
Different files are stored in different ways, depending on their purpose.

! Remember

Remember to back up your files. Turn back to page 21 to learn how to copy files on to storage media.

! Remember

Turn back to Units 112, E20 and 124 for ideas on editing and formatting text files and images.

Sound files

Sound files are used to store music and sound effects. It is now becoming increasingly popular to include music and sound within a website. Types of sound file include:

- A Waveform Audio File (Wave or Wav): a file type suitable for creating sound. Microsoft® and IBM® created this file type in 1991.

- MPEG–1 Audio Layer 3 (MP3): a file format used for digital sounds. You may have an MP3 player, which stores your music in MP3 format.

What do you use to download MP3 files?

Website files

Websites are stored in their own unique file format and must be saved as an HTML file in order for the internet browser to recognise the file as a webpage. As with all software files, you can save, open and name website files. You should always use suitable file names.

! Remember

It is important to consider copyright when using sound files on a website. See pages 28 and 29 for more information on copyright and downloading music.

⊚ Activity: Design a poster

Design a poster to explain about different file types. You should include the following examples:

- text files

- image files

- sound files.

✓ Check

- It is important to use the correct file type when creating webpages.

- Each file should be stored using the smallest amount of space as possible.

Website navigation

Many websites have more than one page. It is important that each page can be found and accessed from other pages within your website.

This can be done by creating links within the page. Links can be a number of different items within the webpage. The experts state that all pages should be only three clicks away. Why do you think this is?

The most common link on a page is simply plain text. The word used would normally represent the new destination. An example of a 'text link' can be seen below:

Primary Schools ▸   Secondary Schools ▸   FE & Vocational ▸

An example of using text as a link to another page

Another way of linking to another page is by using an image. The user will simply click on the image to be directed to another page.

Primary Schools ▸   Secondary Schools ▸   FE & Vocational ▸

An example of using images as a link to another page

The image above shows how images can be used as a link to take the user to another area of the website. The user can click on the images of the individuals to find out more about them. This can enhance the website and limit the amount of text that is needed.

Key term

Link
A connection between two or more web pages.

Functional skills

Reading the text on different websites will help improve your reading skills in **English**.

Activity: Search the Internet

Search the Internet to find a website that uses both text and images as links to navigate to other pages.

✱ Key term

Navigate
To move from one place to another.

✔ Check

- It is important to understand the purpose of each website.

- Each website has a target audience.

Uploading files

Once you have created your different webpages, you need to store them in an appropriate place to ensure your target audience can view the website via the Internet.

There are a number of important checks you need to make before the website goes live on the Internet. You must save the files in HTML format. All images and sound files used for the website also need to be saved in the same folder as the webpages.

Key term

Web server
Where a website 'lives' on the internet.

Activity: Testing

Your webpages need to be tested before they are uploaded. A common problem might be non-working links. Try to think of some more problems you should test for.

Once you are happy that all files have been included, you can then save your files on the allocated web server for the webpages. Normally you would use a hosting company's server to store your files. The hosting company will ensure that the webpage can be viewed on the Internet.

How webpages are stored and how the user of the website views the site

You can see from the diagram above that the website files, including image and sound files, are saved on a server. The server has its own unique address which allows the user of the website to enter the address in their browser to view the site.

Problems with webpages

Websites can be very exciting to look at, but it can become frustrating if you upload a page and the images cannot be seen. There are several potential answers to this problem, including:

- Images are missing from the server. The web designer may have simply forgotten to upload the image files to the server, meaning that the link has been broken.

- Images are too big for the browser to handle quickly. It is important to use the correct file type for images within a website.

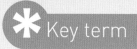
Key term

Upload
To save files onto a website server.

Activity: Review a website

Pick your favourite website. Write a review on the website, making sure to include both the good and bad points about the website.

Check

- Saving files on a server is known as uploading.

- All files used for the website must be uploaded to the server.

ASSESSMENT OVERVIEW

While working through this unit, you will have prepared for completing
the following assessment tasks:

○	1.1 Identify what content and layout will be needed in the webpage	Pages 154–155
○	1.2 Identify the purpose of the webpage and intended audience	Pages 154–155
○	1.3 Select and use a website design template to create a single webpage	Pages 156–157
○	1.4 Enter or insert content for webpages so that it is ready for editing and formatting	Pages 156–157
○	1.5 Organise and combine information needed for webpages	Pages 158–159
○	1.6 Identify copyright and other constraints on using others' information	Pages 158–159
○	1.7 Identify what file types to use for saving content	Pages 160–161
○	1.8 Store and retrieve web files effectively, in line with local guidelines and conventions where available	Pages 160–161
○	2.1 Identify what editing and formatting to use to aid both clarity and navigation	Pages 160–161
○	2.2 Select and use website features to help the user navigate simple websites	Pages 162–163
○	2.3 Use appropriate editing and formatting techniques	Pages 160–161
○	2.4 Check webpages meet needs, using IT tools and making corrections as appropriate	Pages 160–161
○	3.1 Upload content to a website	Pages 164–165
○	3.2 Respond appropriately to common problems when testing a webpage	Pages 164–165

edexcel ⋮⋮⋮

Assignment tips

- Practise using different website creating software.
- Make sure you are clear about who your target audience are before creating your website.
- Experiment with different colours and images on your webpage creations.
- Practise uploading webpages to the Internet.

WORD PROCESSING SOFTWARE

Word processing software has a variety of uses and applications. In the business world, word processing software provides extremely useful tools, such as the creation of letters and memos. In the home, the software provides the facility to write personal letters and create CVs. In education, IT helps develop writing and presentational skills, and also can be used to type and create essays.

In this unit, you will:

- Enter, edit and combine text and other information in documents

- Structure information in documents

- Use word processing software tools to format and present documents

Can you type your name without looking at the keyboard?

Inputting and editing documents

Types of information

Word processing software packages have the capability to present all sorts of different types of information in a variety of different ways. Examples include:

- text
- numbers
- images.

Data input

Information and data can be entered into the document in a number of ways. The most common method used for entering data is to type using a keyboard. Other methods include using voice recognition, a touchscreen or a stylus.

A computer stylus

Shortcuts

Keyboard shortcuts can be used to save time:

Short cut	What it does
Ctrl + N	Opens a new document.
Ctrl + S	Saves the document.
Ctrl + P	Prints the document.

Editing

Any information that is entered into a document can be edited in a number of ways. You can edit the information you wish to change by selecting it and then choosing the required editing tool.

! Remember

When you want to save your word processing files, give them recognisable names so you can easily find and reopen them.

Cut and paste

You can move text or images by 'cutting and pasting':

- Select the information that you wish to move

- Click on the 'Cut' button

- Click where you wish the information to be moved to, and click on the 'Paste' button.

Drag and drop

Alternatively, you can move text or images by 'dragging and dropping':

- Select the information that you wish to move

- Hover over the selected text and hold down the left mouse button. The pointer will change to a packet with a dotted insertion point

- 'Drag' the selected information to a new location and release the left mouse button to 'drop' it.

Undo and delete

- If you edit a document by accident, you can undo the last few changes by clicking on the 'Undo' button

- You can delete information from a document by selecting it, then pressing the 'Delete' button.

Activity: Producing invitations using templates

Find an invitation template in a word processing software package, such as Microsoft Word®. Practise moving around within the template and deleting some text.

* Key term

Template
A document with a pre-set format which can be adapted.

Check

- There are several techniques for editing data in word processing programs.

- You can create new documents using templates if required.

Combining different types of information

It is possible to combine different types of information together in the same document. For example, you can insert a picture from the **clip art** options, add text surrounding the picture and change the order of the text/images.

To insert a picture from clip art, go to 'Insert', then select 'Clip Art'.

You will then see a range of pictures available to use.

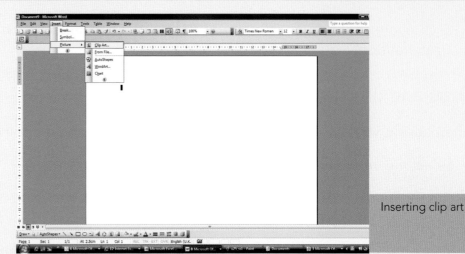

Inserting clip art

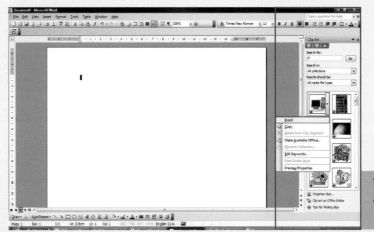

The range of clip art available

Text can be added by clicking anywhere in the document. The way in which images and text are laid out can also changed. This screenshot shows an image which has had text **wrapped** around it.

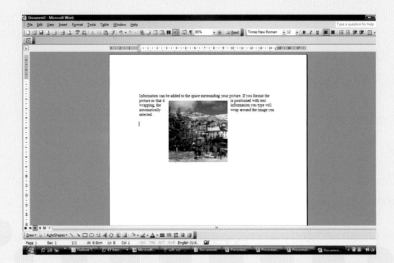

Images can be formatted by double clicking on them and then selecting the required formatting option. The screenshot opposite shows some of the formatting options available for you to use. Why not give them all a try and see how you can make your documents more interesting?

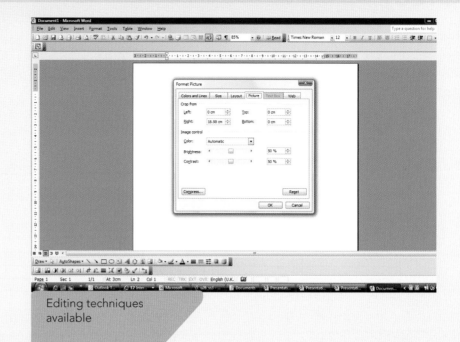

Editing techniques available

You can also change the order of how things appear on the document. For example, you can set the image/text so that one is set behind the other, as shown below.

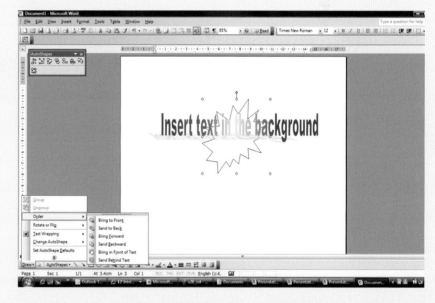

Activity: Try

Try adding a clip art to a word processing document you are working on.

Check

- Clip art and other images can liven up a document.
- You can position the material in a variety of ways.

Key terms

Clip art
A catalogue of images available to use in documents.

Wrapping
The process of limiting material to a particular area.

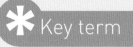
Structuring documents

Creating and modifying tables

It is sometimes useful to present information in **table** form. You can insert a table into a word processing document by selecting 'Insert' then 'Insert Table'. Below, a table has been inserted into a document with five columns and three rows.

Key term

Table
A set of data arranged in rows and columns.

A table

Activity: Inserting tables

Open up a new word processing document and insert a table with five columns and three rows as shown above.

Adding or removing columns

Once you have created a table, you can add or remove rows or columns as required.

To add additional rows or columns to an existing table, right click anywhere on the table, select 'Insert Cells' and then select 'Insert Columns' or 'Insert Rows' as appropriate.

To remove rows or columns, right click on the table and select 'Delete Cells', then select 'Delete entire row' or 'Delete entire column' as appropriate.

Adding a new column to an existing table

Activity: Adding/removing rows and columns

Add an additional row to your table, and remove one of the columns, so that you are left with a table that has four columns and four rows.

Applying heading styles to text

Text can be formatted in many different ways. Word processing software packages provide a number of pre-set heading styles. These can be applied to text in a document. To apply a heading style to your text, simply highlight the text you wish to format, and select the desired style from those available.

Key term

Heading
A term used to describe the subject you are writing about.

Heading style 1	Heading style 2	Heading style 3	Heading style 4	Heading style 5

Different heading styles applied

Activity: Adding headings

Add headings to your table, using an appropriate heading format.

Check

- You can insert and modify tables within a word processing document.

- You can apply heading styles to text.

Formatting tools

The way in which a document needs to be presented will vary depending on the type of document you are trying to create. You want to ensure that the finished document is easy to follow, and focuses the reader's attention.

This screenshot shows the main **formatting** tools used within word processing software packages. These tools can be found on the main toolbar at the top of the screen.

To apply the formatting options, highlight the section of text you wish to format. Then click on the option you want from the ones shown above.

Font style Font size Alignment Highlighting Font colour

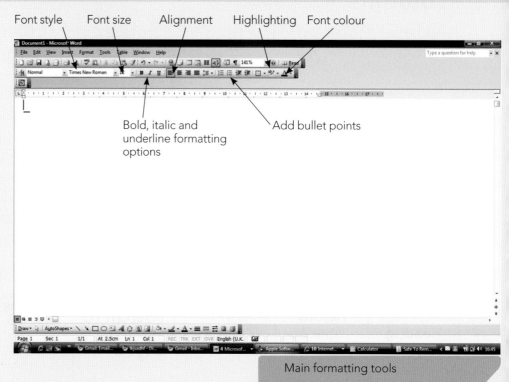

Bold, italic and underline formatting options

Add bullet points

Main formatting tools

Page layout

The way that your page is laid out and printed can be changed. For example, you can choose to lay out a page as either **portrait** or **landscape** by going to 'Page Setup' and selecting the appropriate paper **orientation** as follows:

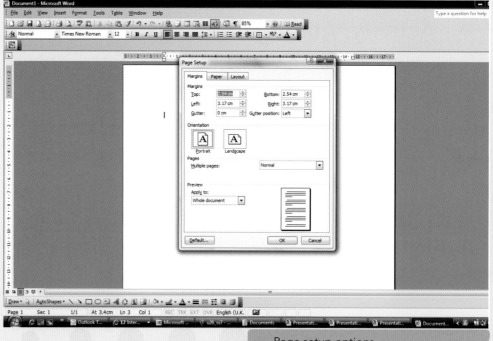

Page setup options

In addition to changing the orientation of the page from portrait to landscape, the size of the paper and margins can also be changed.

How to decide?

The best way to identify how a document needs to be formatted is by having a look at the document using print preview. This will show the whole page on screen, and you can see how balanced the page appears to the reader.

Activity: Opening and editing files

Open the invitation file you created earlier and practise using some of the formatting tools discussed in this topic.

Check

- You can format documents using a variety of tools.
- You can spell check and grammar check documents.

* Key terms

Formatting
The way information is presented.

Portrait
When the vertical dimension of the page is longer than the horizontal.

Landscape
When the horizontal dimension of the page is longer than the vertical.

Orientation
The position of a page – i.e. whether it is portrait or landscape.

! Remember

Always use the spell check and grammar check tools to check your documents.

ASSESSMENT OVERVIEW

While working through this unit, you will have prepared for completing the following assessment tasks:

◯	1.1	Identify what types of information are needed in documents	Pages 168–169
◯	1.2	Identify what templates are available and when to use them	Pages 168–169
◯	1.3	Use keyboard or other input method to enter or insert text and other information	Pages 168–169
◯	1.4	Combine information of different types or from different sources within a document	Pages 170–171
◯	1.5	Enter information into existing tables, forms and templates	Pages 172–173
◯	1.6	Use editing tools to amend document content	Pages 174–175
◯	1.7	Store and retrieve document files effectively, in line with local guidelines and conventions where available	Pages 168–169
◯	2.1	Create and modify tables to organise tabular or numeric information	Pages 172–173
◯	2.2	Select and apply heading styles to text	Pages 172–173
◯	3.1	Identify what formatting to use to enhance presentation of the document	Pages 174–175
◯	3.2	Select and use appropriate techniques to format characters and paragraphs	Pages174–175
◯	3.3	Select and use appropriate page layout to present and print documents	Pages 174–175
◯	3.4	Check documents meet needs, using IT tools and making corrections as appropriate	Pages 174–175

edexcel

Assignment tips

- Practise using word processing software to create different types of documents. You can have a look through the different templates available to give you ideas.
- Experiment with different colours and formatting options.
- Ensure you spell check and grammar check all documents you produce.

THE INTERNET AND WORLD WIDE WEB

The World Wide Web has brought about a revolution. In the last ten years, we have seen the World Wide Web used for shopping (eBay, Amazon), social (MySpace, Facebook), games (Second Life, RuneScape), research (Wikipedia, Encarta Online), maps (Google Streetview, Multimap), videos (YouTube, Google Video), news (BBC, Sky) … and this list is still growing.

The World Wide Web is an incredible resource, one that we have only just begun to fully use. Even now, websites are being developed that will amaze you.

In this unit, you will learn to:

- Explain what the World Wide Web is, how it functions and how we use it

- Understand the basics of the World Wide Web and how it works

- Communicate through the Internet and World Wide Web

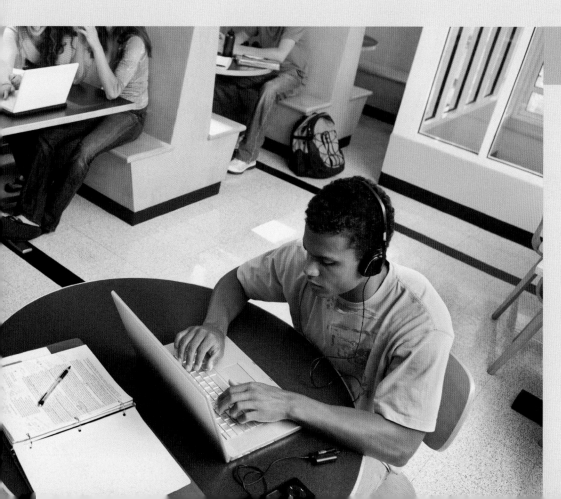

What are *your* favourite websites?

The basics of the Internet

The Internet and the World Wide Web

The Internet is actually very different from the World Wide Web.

The Internet is the 'infrastructure' that allows us to access websites. The Internet includes things like the telephone cables, Internet service providers, modems, the BT local exchange and a few other technical items.

The Internet is used for many different things, including:

- Shopping online
- Reading the news
- Looking at maps
- Playing games
- Socialising with friends
- Researching homework
- Listening to music.

Possibly the most common use of the Internet is for sending email. Approximately 250 billion emails are sent every day – that is almost 3 billion every second!

Another common use is viewing videos. YouTube (owned by Google) is currently the third most visited website in the world, averaging around 24 million visitors per day.

Activity: Most visited websites

In pairs, think of other websites that might figure in the top ten most visited websites.

Discuss as a class, and see if together you can come up with a list of ten.

What do you need to connect to the internet?

In order to connect to the Internet and World Wide Web, you need a few items:

- Computer/laptop/mobile device that is Internet-enabled

- Modem – this allows you to connect to the Internet via a telephone line

- Telephone line (provided by BT or a cable company)

- ISP (Internet Service Provider) – this will 'log' you onto the Internet.

Once you are connected to the Internet, your 'Internet connection' will probably be ADSL (Asymmetric Digital Subscriber Line) – or, in other words, 'broadband'. This is sometimes called an 'always on' connection. Broadband means that you have a very 'broad bandwidth'. Bandwidth refers to the amount of data being downloaded. A broad bandwidth allows you to surf the Internet at much faster speeds.

Another way to connect to the Internet (in the olden days) is through a 'dial-up modem' (56k modem).

However, it is slower. If you watched a video on YouTube using dial-up, it could take two to three minutes to load before it began to play. Using 'broadband', the same video would load almost instantly.

An ADSL router

Key terms

Internet connection
How we connect our devices in order to be able to access webpages.

Bandwidth
How fast our Internet connection is and how much data we can download.

Activity: Group discussion

Can you think of any drawbacks to having to dial up every time you need to use the Internet? Why do you think dial-up Internet is still used even today?

Check

- The Internet is used for communication, business, entertainment, social, travel, news and much more.

- Different bandwidths mean different Internet connection speeds. Dial-up is slow, broadband is faster.

The basics of the World Wide Web

The World Wide Web sits 'on top' of the Internet. The Internet is the foundation/infrastructure of the World Wide Web, and allows us to visit websites.

Think of a street map as the internet. This map allows us to travel to specific houses. Think of houses as websites. If you want to visit your friend's house, you must follow the street map to get there. Without the street map, you wouldn't be able to find the correct house. Each house has a specific address just as each website has a specific address.

URLs

The address of a website is known as a **URL**. URLs are also called domain names. They usually look like this: www.bbc.co.uk.

The format of home addresses can be very different. However, web addresses usually end with either:

- .com

- .co.uk

- .org

- .net

Each website has a unique address (URL). This domain name is simply the address of where the website 'lives' on the Internet.

You live in a building, perhaps a house or flat, but websites live on a web server. This is a computer that is connected to the Internet, just like your home is connected to your street.

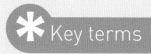

Key terms

URL
A website address.

Web server
Where a website 'lives' o
the Internet.

◎ Activity: Addresses

Ask the person sitting next to you if they know your home address. Then ask them if they know the address of their favourite website (for example, BBC News). Can you think of any other types of domain names? For example, '.org.uk' / '.ac.uk'?

How to find a website

How would you find a website and, more importantly, how would you get there?

In your **web browser**, you simply type the address in the address bar. Many people get confused and type the address of a website into a search engine like Google. The address bar is located at the top of the browser's window, and you will need to type in the full address. For example: www.bbc.co.uk

Key term

Web browser
Software that lets you visit websites (examples include Internet Explorer® and Firefox).

The address bar

Using a search engine

Searching for information is a kind of 'transaction' you can do on the Internet. This is an exchange of information that leads to a result. In this case you find something out.

Search engines are used to search for webpages that you do not know the exact address of. For example, if we didn't know the BBC's website address, we could do a search on a search engine such as Google.

The search would need to include key words about the website, i.e. 'BBC' or 'British Broadcasting Corporation'.

Activity: Internet search

What 'key words' would you type into Google to find the winners of the Premier League 2010, or perhaps who is number 1 in the music charts now? Try it.

Check

- The World Wide Web is websites.
- Domain names are basically street addresses, but for websites.

What is email?

Electronic mail, or '**email**' for short, is the same as sending a handwritten letter and then posting it. The difference is how you write the letter and how it is sent.

The letter is written digitally (on your computer) and the recipient (the person you are sending it to) receives it on their computer.

A handwritten letter is delivered to an address by a postman. Without an address on the letter, the postman wouldn't know where to deliver it. An electronic mail also needs an address – or, to be exact, an electronic mailing address (email address).

Activity: Group discussion

Here are some popular email account providers:

- Hotmail
- Gmail
- YahooMail.

Ask your classmates what type of email account they use. Is it on the list above?

Within your email, you will have an address book to store all of the email addresses you use frequently. Email addresses are often long, complicated and easily forgotten. It's a good idea to keep them in an address book so you don't forget them.

Managing your email messages

You can also organise your emails into folders. Deleting emails you don't want is a simple click away. Also, because email is digital, you can copy and paste their contents into other files.

Spam (junk email from unwanted people) is a problem, but most email providers such as Gmail and Hotmail provide a 'Spam' button, which allows you to stop unwanted emails from that sender.

✱ Key term

Electronic mail/email
Similar to a handwritten letter, but sent digitally.

! Remember

Use your address book as much as you can.

Managing folders

Case study:
Parveen's spam problem

Parveen has an email account. He uses it about once a week to read emails from friends. Recently he has found that every time he opens the account there are loads of emails from strange email addresses, including ones that seem to come from his own email account!

Parveen is really suspicious and deletes all the messages straightaway. He has heard about how you can get viruses by opening emails like this. But the emails keep coming and eventually Parveen stops using the account.

Activity: Dealing with spam

What do you think Parveen could have done to deal with the spam problem?

Activity: Organise your emails

If you have an email account, choose one of the things you have learnt in this topic, such as using your address book, and use this to make your own email account more organised.

✓ Check

- Emails are sent just like letters. They have an address (email), and are delivered electronically through the Internet.

Writing an email

When you 'compose' an email, you must specify to whom you are sending the message 'to'.

The email address must be spelt correctly, otherwise it may not get to its destination.

The subject line should be a brief introduction to what the email is about. For example, 'Urgent' or 'Hello Mum'.

The main content is where you write your email, just as you would a normal letter. Don't forget to click 'send' when you're ready. (Many email providers allow you to save your email, so you can send it later.)

You can add more than one recipient, which is a massive advantage over traditional letters. You can also add a 'secret' recipient by using BCC (Blind Carbon Copy).

Netiquette

Netiquette is important when writing email.

Key term

Netiquette
Rules for how to write in emails and on the Internet.

Activity: Netiquette

Do U Fink the way I av wrote dis line is alr8?

Can you rewrite this into a sentence that would be appropriate for an email/letter?

When using CAPITALS online, it is interpreted as SHOUTING. Large text can also be misunderstood as shouting too, and writing in large font can sometimes be seen as being rude.

Emoticons

Emoticons are used to help show the reader how you feel.

- :P means you are joking
- :D means you are laughing
- :) means you are smiling
- ;) means you are winking

Some computer programs will automatically change these into a picture.

Activity: Internet slang

Think of as many examples of Internet slang as you can, such as 'lol' ('laugh out loud'). Now make a list of the times when you shouldn't use this in an email – for example, in an email to a customer.

Check

- Emails are sent just like letters. They have an address (email), and are delivered electronically through the Internet.

- Netiquette is important when writing an email. Make sure you use appropriate language, depending on who you are writing to.

Communication methods on the Internet

Communication on the Internet has changed over time. First there were text-only **web pages**, then email, and, today, there many different ways to communicate.

Way of communicating	What is it?	Advantages
Forum	**Online communities** where you can share information.	You can get help and advice, even for technical problems.
Social networking	A network like Facebook, Bebo or MySpace.	Makes it easy to stay in touch with friends.
Blogs	A little like a diary. You can tell people what you are doing.	A good way to share what's going on in your life.
Instant messaging	Messages that are sent and received instantly (for example, MSN Messenger, YahooChat).	Much faster than email.
Publishing webpages	A way to put information on the Internet.	You can be quite creative and there is lots of software to help you (for example, Adobe® Dreamweaver® or Microsoft FrontPage®).

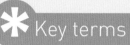

Key terms

Instant messaging
Short text-like messages that are sent over the internet and received instantly.

Online communities
Communities of people who share the same interests as each other.

Webpages
Pages on the Internet that make up the World Wide Web.

! Remember

When using social networking sites, be careful of how much and what information you publish.

What websites or software do you use to communicate online?

Activity: Creating your own webpage

If you were to create a webpage, what would it be about? Have a look at the topics below, or think of your own list:

- Education
- Fun
- Games
- News
- Sport.

Activity: Problem solving

If you had a problem with your computer, what would you do first of all?

- Ask a friend
- Search on the Internet
- Look for professional help?

Check

You have learnt:

- Communication via the Internet is very common.
- Online communities allow you to share and find useful information.
- You need to be careful about what personal information you give out online.

ASSESSMENT OVERVIEW

While working through this unit, you will have prepared for completing the following assessment tasks:

○	1.1	Describe the uses of the Internet	Pages 178–179
○	1.2	Identify the requirements for an Internet connection	Pages 178–179
○	1.3	Identify the features of two types of Internet connections	Page 178–179
○	1.4	Relate the term bandwidth to types of internet connections	Page 178–179
○	2.1	Describe the components of the Web	Page 180
○	2.2	Explain how web addresses work	Pages 180–181
○	2.3	Explore websites by using a browser	Pages 180–181
○	2.4	Search for reliable information on the Web	Page 181
○	3.1	Explain how email works	Page 182
○	3.2	Write and send email messages	Pages 184–185
○	3.3	Manage email messages	Pages 182–183
○	3.4	Identify correct email etiquette	Pages 184–185
○	4.1	Identify the features of online communities	Page 186
○	4.2	Explain how instant messaging works	Pages 186–187
○	4.3	Explain how to create and publish webpages	Pages 186–187

edexcel

Assignment tips

- Remember that the Internet is different from the World Wide Web.
- Stay safe online: be careful about what personal information you post on the Internet. You never know who will read it.
- Treat your emails as formal letters, and remember your netiquette.
- Avoid using slang and abbreviations in your email.

DIGITAL LIFESTYLE
UNIT E51

A digital lifestyle is not as futuristic as you might think. In fact, we are living one right now.

Being digital has many advantages and, with technology improving all the time, we have access to amazing and wonderful gadgets that enable us to work and play in new and unique ways.

Technology in the world is changing at a very fast pace. As technology changes, so does the way we live in that world.

In this unit, you will learn:

- The basics of digital technology, and how it is used in digital devices

- The basics of creating and recording digital audio

- The basics of creating and recording digital video

- The basics of digital photography

- Opportunities that technology brings, including career and life choices

What does the phrase 'digital devices' mean to you?

Basics of digital technology

Digital technology exists in almost every aspect of our lives:

- Digital television (Freeview, satellite)

- DVD movies (Blu-ray, DVD disc)

- MP3 players (iPod, Zune)

- Mobile phones (iPhone, BlackBerry®)

- Laptops (Dell, Mac).

Benefits

There are many benefits of leading a digital lifestyle.

Feature	Benefit
Portable	If you are always on the go, you are able to take your digital life with you.
Flexible mobile devices	You can access lots of different software on the move.
Social	Social networking websites allow you to share videos and photos. Email allows you to communicate.
On demand	Information is available on demand, thanks to search engines and online encyclopaedias.

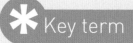

Key term

Benefits
Improvements due to using technological devices.

Activity: Group discussion

Can you imagine life without your mobile phone? Think how many text messages you send every day.

Video game technology has also exploded. You are now able to use your games console over the Internet. This means you can now play someone on your favourite game, on the other side of the world.

Handheld video games have also become very popular, with consoles such as PSPs and Nintendo DS™s becoming almost as widely used as PlayStations and the Xbox.

Using the Nintendo Wii™.
An example of digital
technology.

Digital devices

Digital devices come in many shapes and sizes. They include:

- Digital cameras

- Digital videos

- PDAs (Personal Digital Assistants)

- Games consoles

- Mobile phones.

Technology has enabled these devices to get faster, smaller and cheaper.

Key term

Digital devices
Devices such as cameras,
mobile phones.

Activity: Digital devices

How many digital devices do you own? Does your mobile device do
all of the above?

Check

- Sharing data is much easier when it is digital.

- Digital technology is used through different devices.

Basics of digital audio

What is digital audio?

Audio is usually in analogue format. This is how our ears listen to sound, and how sound is created.

Digital audio is analogue sound, converted into digital format.

Changing audio into digital

We can do this by:

- Using audio editing software

- Recording speech onto a computer using a microphone.

The audio editing software will compress the file size of the audio. This makes the file size very small and allows us to store many songs on our MP3 player.

◎ **Activity: Digital audio format**

What digital audio format do you use to put music onto your iPod/MP3 player? Do you know how many songs you can store on your music-playing device?

Output formats

Once we have recorded or created our digital audio file, we can put it onto our digital devices. These include:

- iPods/MP3 players

- Audio CDs (played on a CD player)

- DVDs (can store many more files than a CD).

Streaming, such as from websites like YouTube, means that music can be downloaded and played, but no file is ever saved. It allows music to be played directly from websites, without having to wait.

Which of the digital devices listed do you use most often?

File sizes

Here are some different file sizes that are commonly used:

File size	What it may contain
Very large file 1 GB (1,024MB)	High-quality movie download.
Large file 0.5GB (512MB)	Movie download; game demo.
Medium file 50MB	MP3 audio CD download.
Small file 10MB	A 30-second video clip.
Extra small file 5MB	A high quality 5-minute MP3 music file.

Activity: Output devices

Which output device allows the most amount of digital audio to be stored? (HINT: Look at the sizes.)

- DVD (4.7GB)
- CD (650MB)
- iPod (120GB).

Check

- Digital audio is analogue sound, converted into digital format.
- When you are streaming, no file is actually saved on your computer.

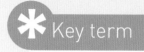
Basics of digital video

Video used to be recorded using tapes (analogue), but the growth of technology has now made it affordable to record video straight onto DVDs, or onto a memory card.

To do this people use:

- Digital video recorders
- Digital cameras
- Mobile phones.

Which format?

Format	Use
AVI	Most common format.
.MPEG	Used to compress a very large digital video file to make it smaller.
FLV	Small format to allow people to stream from websites (for example, YouTube).

When may you use digital video?

◎ Activity: Recording video on your mobile phone

Check to see if your mobile phone can record video. If it has a camera, there is a good chance it can record video too.

Editing

Videos can be edited digitally. **Video editing** allows you to:

- Remove parts of a video

- Add titles, subtitles or insert still images, or perhaps a background song

- Create your own DVD movie.

Key term

Video editing
Editing the video such as removing frames, and adding titles.

Activity: Research

How would you go about making a holiday video for YouTube using the techniques above?

Features of web video technologies

Web videos allow people to:

- Share and comment on videos online

- Watch videos immediately, without having to wait for the whole file to download onto their computer

- Hold video conferences and video calls with someone else over the Internet (for example, Skype).

Activity: Research

Which web video technologies do you use the most?

✓ Check

- You can record digital video straight onto some digital devices.

- You can edit your videos and share them in a number of ways.

Digital photography

The features of digital cameras

Photography is a real passion for some people. It allows you to capture a moment, and express yourself. Nowadays you can use a digital camera, which allows you to:

- See what you are about to photograph on the camera screen

- Review and delete any photographs you do not want

- Take thousands of photographs (depending on memory card size)

- Use digital settings to help improve the quality of photographs

- Download and **edit** images on a computer to improve them.

The memory card

Most digital cameras use a **memory card** to store images, such as:

- SD Memory Card

- XD Memory Card

- Compact Flash Memory Card.

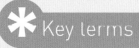

Key terms

Edit
To change something (perhaps changing text, a photo or a spreadsheet).

Memory card
Used to store digital photos captured by a digital camera.

This is how a USB cable connects to a computer.

A digital camera simply records an image from its lens, and stores it in digital format (JPEG) on the camera's memory card. These images can then be downloaded onto a computer using a USB cable.

Activity: Memory cards

What memory card does your digital camera or mobile phone use?

Editing images

Once you have your digital image on your computer, you can edit many parts of a photo. For example, if the photo was taken in low light, you can improve the lightness and contrast.

Printers

All printers have different features and abilities. Here are a few:

- Allow digital camera memory cards to slot straight into the printer and printing from it

- Print fast, or with better colour

- Ink/inkjet-based or laser-based (usually more expensive).

Activity: Research

Find a printer at college, school or at home and see if you can work out its main features.

Check

- Digital cameras store most images on their memory card.

- You can edit and improve digital images once you put them on your computer.

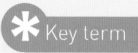

Career opportunities

As technology expands, **career opportunities** grow. Many people now work from home, mainly thanks to the Internet and digital communication. Being able to hold video meetings, send emails and send files has now made this a possible job choice.

Activity: IT at work

Think of someone you know, and how they use IT at their job. (Note: IT is not just about using a computer.) Examples might include:

- Shop workers using barcode scanners

- Taxi drivers using Sat Nav (GPS)

- Estate agents taking pictures of houses using digital cameras.

Why are barcodes used in shops?

Career opportunities

Think of the latest communication devices, such as the iPhone. All of the applications that you can use on the iPhone have been designed by **IT professionals**. IT professionals include:

- Game designers (game applications)

- Web designers (websites you visit)

- Programmers (applications that perform advanced tasks)

- Digital artists (applications that use graphics and cartoons).

Don't think that any of this is out of your reach. If you can use a computer, the next step is to develop an area of your interest, and continue studying within it.

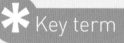

Functional skills

Learning the different meaning of 'IT professionals' and 'IT developers' will improve your skills in **English**.

Developers

IT developers are professionals who specialise in developing software. As with the iPhone, developers are people who design a software, and then continually develop it to improve it. By developing something, it should get better and better.

Case study:
Google Maps

Google Maps started out simply showing maps with street names. It was then developed to allow users to zoom in and out of areas. Following this IT developers thought, let's add some images to make it look realistic, which led to the 'Satellite View' feature.

Then the developers thought, I wonder if we could put pictures in at street level, which gave us the 'Street View' feature. This allows the user to zoom in and pan across, as if they were standing there. You can now 'stand' in Tokyo city centre – as if you were actually there!

IT developers developed this software from something very basic, to the advanced and quite amazing tool that many people use frequently today.

Activity: IT development
What other things could a developer work on improving?

Check
- IT professionals are professionals who work within the IT industry.
- IT developers are IT professionals who develop and continually improve things like software.

ASSESSMENT OVERVIEW

While working through this unit, you will have prepared for completing
the following assessment tasks:

○	1.1	Describe the benefits of digital technology	Pages 190–191
○	1.2	Explain how digital technology expands the features of digital devices	Pages 190–191
○	2.1	Identify the characteristics of digital audio	Pages 192–193
○	2.3	Explain the concepts of recording, copying and converting digital audio	Pages 192–193
○	2.4	Identify the features of speech technologies	Pages 192–193
○	3.1	Identify the characteristics of digital video	Pages 194–195
○	3.2	Explain what digital video editing is and the output formats for digital video	Pages 194–195
○	3.3	Identify the features of web video technologies	Pages 194–195
○	4.1	Explain the benefits, features and workings of a digital camera	Pages 196–197
○	4.2	Explain how to edit and manage digital images	Pages 196–197
○	4.3	Identify the features of different types of printers that are available for printing photos	Pages 196–197
○	5.1	Explain how digital technology helps people work from any location	Pages 198–199
○	5.2	Identify the career opportunities available for information workers	Pages 198–199
○	5.3	Identify the career opportunities available for IT professionals	Pages 198–199
○	5.4	Identify the career opportunities available for developers	Pages 198–199

edexcel :::

Assignment tips

- When you are recording any digital media (photo, audio or video), ensure your memory card is large enough to fit it all on.
- Check your digital devices are fully charged. You don't want to run out of battery when recording.
- When editing videos, you need a powerful computer. If your computer is slow, be patient.
- Don't forget to make back-up copies of any digital files. You can always revert back to these if necessary.

Glossary

Accessibility – Helping people with difficulties use a computer more easily.

Accuracy – The level of how closely something matches its required state.

Acquire image – How you 'get' your image onto your computer.

Address book – A virtual book that stores details such as email addresses.

Advice – Information from someone who has greater knowledge about something.

Alignment – The position of material on a page.

Animation – A series of pictures put together to create a seamless and smooth moving picture.

Attachment – A file that is attached and sent within an email.

Automated routine – A pre-recorded event that will occur when a certain action is performed (for example, a press of a button).

Bandwidth – How fast our Internet connection is and how much data we can download.

Benefits – Improvements due to using technological devices.

Bias – When someone's point of view influences what they say or write about something.

Blog – A diary-like website, in which you can write and share anything you like.

Career opportunities – Opportunities for jobs and employment.

Caution – Taking care when reading and replying to emails.

Cell (spreadsheet) – An individual square within a spreadsheet.

Chatroom – A virtual room on the Internet where people can 'chat' to each other.

Checklist – A list of items required or needed for the project.

Clearing – Deleting information (for example, from the cell of a spreadsheet).

Clip art – A catalogue of images available to use in documents.

Column (spreadsheet) – Cells that are positioned next to each other in a vertical line.

Communication – Interaction between two or more people or devices.

Compose – To write an email.

Confidentiality – Keeping personal and private information safe.

Constraints – Rules that we are not allowed to break.

Contact – Someone you know and interact with electronically.

Crop – A tool to choose an area of an image, and throw away the rest of the image.

Cut and paste – To digitally 'cut' something and then 'paste' it somewhere else.

Cyber-bullying – The same as bullying, but carried out via the Internet.

Data – Information, often combines both numbers and letters.

Digital audio – Audio (sound) that is now in digital form.

Digital devices – Devices such as cameras, mobile phones.

Digital file – A file that is created when you create and save work on a computer.

Digital video – Video that has been recorded and converted for use on computers.

Display settings – Changing a display, to suit your personal preferences, such as brightness, contrast, size.

Distribution list – Similar to an address book, but with pre-selected entries within the address book so that you can quickly and easily send the same email to everyone within the list.

Dongle – An electronic device that is plugged into the computer to allow a copy-protected program to run.

DSL – A telephone line that has special equipment which allows it to receive information from the Internet, or send information at very high speeds.

Edit – To change something (perhaps changing text, a photo or a spreadsheet).

Electronic mail/email – Similar to a handwritten letter, but sent digitally.

Enter – To place something (for example, information) in a particular place (for example, a cell).

File format – What type of file is used for digital work.

File type – Different files are stored in different ways, depending on their purpose.

Folder – A digital folder that helps you to organise digital files on a computer.

Form – A series of 'fields' that allow you to type in information, and then send off the form (for example, a comment form).

Formatting – The way information is presented.

Formula – A sequence of commands that make a sum (for example, in spreadsheets).

Graphic – Any digital file that is a picture or illustration.

Grooming – Trying to take advantage of young or vulnerable people online.

Guidelines – Suggestions about how to do things.

Handouts – Printouts of slides for your audience to read as you give your presentation, or keep for future reference.

Hardware – The physical parts of a computer that you need in order to be able to connect to the Internet.

Heading – A term used to describe the subject you are writing about.

Health and safety – Making sure that people are safe when using a computer.

House style – Set colours, logos and fonts used by an organisation.

Icon – A simple picture that indicates a program or a command.

Image editing software – The software used to edit and manipulate your acquired image.

Imperative – Very important and essential.

Information – Knowledge gained through study, experience or instruction.

Input – How information is put into a computer.

Instant messaging – Short text-like messages that are sent over the Internet and received instantly.

Internet connection – How we connect our devices in order to be able to access webpages.

Internet Service Provider (ISP) – A company that allows you to connect to the Internet.

IT developers – Specific professionals who work in developing IT software.

IT professionals – People who work in IT industries.

IT system – A process that is run and operated by a computer.

JPEG – A file format used for photographic images.

Key words – The most important terms or phrases.

Landscape – When the horizontal dimension of the page is longer than the vertical.

Layout – How you lay out the contents of your DTP design.

Link – A connection between two or more webpages.

Log in – Logging into a computer or system with an individual user name and password.

Maintenance – Cleaning, checking, improving, modifying to ensure something continues to work properly.

Manipulate – To alter something, such as an image's size, position or layout.

Margin – The area between the text and the edge of the page.

Memory card – Used to store digital photos captured by a digital camera.

Mobile device (also known as a 'handheld device') – A small computing device, such as a mobile phone.

Modem – A piece of electronic equipment that allows information from one computer to be sent along telephone wires to another computer.

Navigate – To move from one place to another.

Navigation – The routes you can use to explore a website.

Netiquette – Rules for how to write in emails and on the Internet.

Number – A value between 0 and 9. A number can be any size.

Online communities – Communities of people who share the same interests as each other.

Organise – To put things in a sensible order to make things easier for yourself.

Orientation – The position of a page – i.e. whether it is portrait or landscape.

Output – How a computer gives out information.

Phishing – A scam email designed to trick you into giving passwords and account details.

Physical stress – When the body is under constant use, which could cause harm or injury.

Plan – To work out what you need to do before you do it.

Podcasts – A series of short video/audio clips containing information on a topic.

Portrait – When the vertical dimension of the page is longer than the horizontal.

Presentation – The appearance of an object.

Procedures – Steps you would take to do something.

Proportion – Keeping things within the same dimension as they were originally.

Publishing – Completing and finalising a product for a customer, such as a newsletter or website.

Purpose – The reason behind doing something (for example, an IT system creating a website).

Relevant – Having a bearing on or connection with the subject.

Respond – Replying to an email.

Review – To investigate something and give an opinion on the results.

Risk – Potential threats to people's safety.

Row (spreadsheet) – Cells that are positioned next to each other in a horizontal line.

Screen resolution – How much detail is displayed on a computer monitor.

Search engine – A program that searches documents for keywords and returns a list of the documents where the keywords were found.

Search query/criteria – The text you type into a search engine to find webpages.

Search results – Results (websites) that are found by a search engine when you type in your search text.

Secure connection – A safe channel to pass data from one device to another.

Select – To find and choose an item.

Shapes – Simple shapes that are used to help improve images, such as magazine covers.

Sim card – A chip card that is inserted into a mobile phone, which contains all the owner's data.

Slide – A single page of a presentation.

Slideshow – The way in which the slides will appear during a presentation.

Software – The applications you use on your computer.

Sort – To arrange data in a suitable order.

Spam – Unwanted emails, often trying to sell something.

Specification – A list of requirements that are used to create and complete a project.

Spell checker – Software that will check what you have typed, looking for spelling and grammatical errors.

Storage media – Allows users to store folders and files outside the computer.

Streamline – To ensure that different elements of a business work together in a smoother and more efficient manner.

Styles – Predefined text formatting, consisting of certain fonts, sizes, colours, etc.

Stylus – A small pen-shaped instrument used with a computer screen.

Synchronisation – Two mobile devices transferring information between each other.

Table – A set of data arranged in rows and columns.

Target audience – The people who are most likely to use a website.

Task – A specific piece of work required to be completed, such as an assignment.

Techniques – Using the tools available within the software to complete a task.

Template – A document with a preset format which can be adapted.

Test – To ensure a product works as it is designed to.

Text – Any letter, number or character. Or a combination of all three.

Text box – Enables the user to input text information into a software program.

Text flow – How text wraps and flows around an image

Text tool – A tool in your image editing software that lets you 'type' text over an image.

Tools – The tools within your image editing software. These allow you to manipulate your photo.

Upload – To save files onto a website server.

URL – A website address.

User interface – Software to enable/help users to work with a computer.

Video editing – Editing the video such as removing frames, and adding titles.

Virus – A file that can cause disruption and harm to your computer.

Web browser – Software that lets you visit websites (examples include Internet Explorer® and Firefox®).

Webpages – Pages on the Internet that make up the World Wide Web.

Web server – Where a website 'lives' on the Internet.

Wi-fi – A way of connecting computers or other electronic machines to a network by using radio signals rather than wires.

Website template – The outline of a webpage that has been created previously.

Wrapping – The process of limiting material to a particular area.

Zoom – Being able to make a digital object larger, by 'zooming' in and seeing it more clearly.

Index